THOR RAMSEY

A COMEDIAN'S GUIDE TO THEOLOGY

Regal

From Gospel Li
Ventura, Californi

Published by Regal
From Gospel Light
Ventura, California, U.S.A.
www.regalbooks.com
Printed in the U.S.A.

Library of Congress Cataloging-in-Publication Data
Ramsey, Thor.
    A comedian's guide to theology / Thor Ramsey.
        p. cm.
    ISBN-13: 978-0-8307-4530-2 (trade paper)
    1. Apologetics—Miscellanea. 2. Apologetics—Humor. 3. Theology—Miscellanea. 4. Theology—Humor. 5. Christianity—Miscellanea. 6. Christianity—Humor. I. Title.
    BT1103.R36 2007
    230.02'07—dc22

                                                                    2007033632

1 2 3 4 5 6 7 8 9 10 / 10 09 08

Rights for publishing this book outside the U.S.A. or in non-English languages are administered by Gospel Light Worldwide, an international not-for-profit ministry. For additional information, please visit www.glww.org, email info@glww.org, or write to Gospel Light Worldwide, 1957 Eastman Avenue, Ventura, CA 93003, U.S.A.

If this thing doesn't sell, this may be my one and only chance, so . . .
I'd like to dedicate this book to Dinika and Eden. I love you both.
Officially and in print.

Contents

If you care about Truth at all, then you should buy this book, because the truth is, I need the money. Even if you don't care about Truth, then buy this book if you care about kids, because I have a lovely seven-year-old daughter who will one day need braces. I'm sorry to pose a moral dilemma if you happen to be browsing at the bookstore, but if you put this book down now you're basically turning your back on a child.

The importance of Truth is obvious, because it is capitalized. Presently, there is a crisis of Truth within the evangelical Church. People keep saying that we are on a journey to a new era, the postmodern era. Well, wake me up when we get there. It's not that I don't care about postmodernism, it's just that I have to take Dramamine on long trips, and it makes me drowsy.

The idea of Truth is being assaulted from many different angles. Allow me to illustrate the problem, since I have a laptop and am writing a book. When I was a child, my sister once said to me, "Mom said to clean your room." I told her, "I believe you're misquoting my mother." Whenever someone says something you don't like, just claim they're being misquoted. This guy named Bart Ehrman wrote a book titled *Misquoting Jesus* because, apparently, Jesus told him to clean his room. Bart is a former youth group member who now makes a living weakening the faith of believers and their pets. (I can only assume that the pets inherit the faith of their guardians.) He's a former evangelical, a lapsed insider now attacking the faith from without. I just think he's an enlarged apostate, which I believe means that he has to go to the bathroom a lot.

I also read a book by Sam Harris, an atheist who more than resembles Ben Stiller. His book is called *The End of Faith*, which basically says, "Muslims want to blow people up because of their holy book, the Koran. Christianity and Judaism have a holy book too, so they shouldn't be let off the hook just because they haven't killed anyone in the last thousand years. You should embrace rationalism and treat other people nice because . . . well, the Golden Rule is a good thing." Sam tells me to abandon my faith, and all he has for me at the end is the Golden Rule? Buddy, that's already ours. So, really, I'm right back where I started.

Sam is trying to attack the faith, but mostly he just makes journalists feel better about being anti-religious. (My apologies to journalists who aren't anti-religious, but unfortunately for you, comedy works best with sweeping generalities.)

It's the assault on Truth from within the Church that currently concerns me. (Yes, I'm out to save the essentials of Christianity. You can thank me later.) You see, in case you've forgotten from four paragraphs ago, we're entering the postmodern era, which means bellbottoms are really out of style. Or not. The thing is, you can't say with any certainty that bellbottoms are out of style, because the very nature of Truth is being questioned . . . unless the truth happens to be how much you have to pay for the bellbottoms. Then Truth is pretty absolute. Even at these outlet malls, the cashiers don't seem to be embracing postmodernism.

It is often said that it doesn't matter what you believe as long as you're sincere. My mother-in-law believes that I'm an idiot. Well, okay, sometimes you can be sincere and right. But my point is, what if she had been wrong? You see? Sometimes sincerity doesn't change the Truth.

Lots of people, myself included, believe that Truth is an unchanging reality that doesn't alter whether you do or don't like it or agree with it. If a comedian isn't funny, the emcee will go up after his set and ask the crowd, "Well, did you at least like his shoes?" That's the traditional view of Truth. It corresponds with reality.

There is another view of truth within the Church now, and it's not capitalized. That shows you how serious things have become. The new view of truth espoused by many prominent writers, thinkers and pastors is that we are trapped in the language of our particular cultures. Thus communication between various people groups becomes difficult because we all have ways of saying things that are particular to our group. The question is, If words aren't reliable, then why should we listen to anything these people have to say? Now, I don't want to bore you with a heady and scholarly argument against this idea of being trapped inside language, so let me just give you the gist of the counterargument: That's stupid. There. That pretty much sums it up. Did you understand me? You did? That's because we're not trapped inside of language.

Some of these Christian leaders are part of a young movement in evangelicalism called *the emerging church*, which I will explain below. Now, I consider myself part of the emerging church, but I'm emerging more along the lines of people like John Burke, though he is much nicer than I am; Shane Claiborne, minus the influence of male pattern baldness; and Mark Driscoll, without his tenacious Calvinism—all people that I will not explain below. But I'm probably only part of the emerging church because I cannot bring myself to wear a tie. (If you're wearing a tie and you tell someone you're a Christian, they think you're Mormon.)

Here's the part where I explain below. (It means beneath or lower.)

Okay, if you're not familiar with the emerging church, just ask anyone who considers himself (or herself) part of the movement and that person will explain it to you in around a billion words. They don't want to be boxed in, so they define it until you either kill them or kill yourself, which can really put a damper on emerging. Generally, emerging Christians can be found wherever there is a group of disgruntled white guys. Rather than biblical exposition, most emerging Christians prefer blended coffee. Proponents of the emerging church shy away from dogma and such ideas as proclaiming Christ as exclusive Lord and Savior, which is really encouraging to the Persecuted Church around the world where Christians are still being killed for their faith. The emerging church also practices loving tolerance, especially if you throw around buzzwords like "generous," "missional," "relational," "authentic," "narrative" and "conversation." When participating in an emerging church service, avoid throwing around words like "heresy," which they are less tolerant of.

The Emergent Church movement seeks to appeal to postmodern people by denying *most* biblical truth. Okay, that was exaggerating the problem, so let me state it this way: The emerging church seeks to appeal to postmodern people by denying *lots* of biblical truth. There. That's more accurate. Members of the emerging church want to bridge the divide between conservative evangelicals and mainline denominations, because mainline churches still have potlucks. And who doesn't like a good casserole?

Much of the emerging church has to do with appealing to young people who don't like to be told what to do in the first place, not that grandma's a pushover. So, this idea that Truth is fuzzy is really appealing to them.

No matter how culturally relevant we become, there are still things that people will hate about Christianity. If we lose the things that really get people's goat, then what fun is there in practicing our religion? Historic Christianity is in a dangerous place when we lose the ability to upset people's livestock. There are things essential to Christianity that we cannot redefine or reimagine, but we can fit them nicely on a bumper sticker. "Honk if you're going to hell." "Honk if you're with someone who is going to hell!" "Jesus is my copilot. I'm sorry he just cut you off." It's the Incarnation for a nation of cars.

This book is reactionary in nature, which is really what being a fundamentalist Christian is all about. Though I don't consider myself a fundamentalist Christian, I do believe there are fundamentals that are essential to Christian orthodoxy, so I imagine that at some point you'll call me a fundamentalist and I'll just have to live with it. If you must call me something (no, besides that), call me an Emergent essentialist and then give me credit for coining a phrase.

Maybe I'm just *nuevo* fundamentalist. For instance, the traditional fundamentalist Christian thinks you're going to hell if you smoke. I don't think you're going to hell if you smoke. You're just going to heaven faster. Still, the promising thing about fundamentalist Christianity is that there are no bombs involved. Fundamentalist Christians might make you feel bad by judging you, but generally they won't blow you up.

Generally.

I feel the need to address those of you who may be offended by my jokes about fundamentalist Christians bombing things, as I'll be addressing various possibly offended readers throughout this book. So, regarding my jokes about Christian bombings: (1) We have to face up to the fact that a few fundamentalist Christians, however misguided, have bombed abortion clinics; (2) you can use the Bible to categorically condemn such bombings; (3) our bombing stats are still way lower than Muslims, so we're still good.

In my heart of hearts, I feel this is a book that had to be written, primarily because I've already spent the advance for said book.

Most of the stories in this book will have to do with me, and I'd like to apologize for that but, hey, it's my book. I can't write stories about you, because I don't know you. Not that I wouldn't mind hanging out, but make an effort, man. You never call. Any errors in this book, I'd like to take credit for, but unfortunately, most of my ideas are based on what other people have already written, so really it's their fault.

Thor Ramsey
September 2007
Undisclosed Think Tank,
Half Empty

(Because Postmoderns Need Their Choices)

It's only after you become a Christian—the born-again variety who experiences a conversion, with corresponding voting habits—that you begin to hem and haw about explaining your beliefs. Maybe you're one of those people. Maybe you're annoyed by one of those people and would like to understand them better. And in understanding, you hope, maybe they will annoy you less. Maybe you don't want to know what they believe because you're afraid you might become one of them.

Not all Christians are annoying, only the ones who make national headlines. Christians you've never heard of—salt of the earth. Famous believers—if they would only shut-up.[1]

Explaining the nuances of what Christians believe about God is known as theology. For some reason, this is less offensive in written form. In the form of the person sitting next to you on a plane, it's very offensive. On a recent flight, I was sitting quietly, reading my Bible, when the old man sitting next to me piped up and said, "The first 450 pages of the Bible are crap." *Okay, sir, I'll see you in chapter 9.*

"But still," you may object, "why cover the essentials of Christian theology with humor, something Christians haven't been noted for having in the first place?"

---

1. Or quit having affairs. Or stay married.

I would like to answer that. Far be it from me to snub a question after putting words in your mouth. First, your basic theological book strings together words into sentences like "Coherentism and pragmatism overcome metaphysical realism with modernist epistemology." I use words like "stripper" and "crap."[2] This makes the loftiness of theology much more accessible to bouncers.

Laughter is a sign of humility, from a Christian standpoint anyway. If you can't laugh at yourself, it's a sign that you might be choking on something. Put this book down and have someone slap you hard on the back. There. You see? You coughed up "taking yourself too seriously" all over the floor.

Second, my extremely good friend, as a comedian of faith who visits at least two different cities weekly, I have performed for denominations ranging from Charismatic Episcopalians, to Ted Haggard's church (one week after his public fall); to a struggling congregation in Ukiah, California, that meets in what was once the Reverend Jim Jones's church; to respectable Reformed churches and booming Baptist congregations; to an all-black church in New Orleans that had a garage full of expensive cars.

Who says Christians aren't funny?

Christians have always been funny, just not on purpose.

Yet, if you need an even better reason for the necessity of a comedy routine on current theological thought, consider the following description of the evangelical Church. In his book *The Culturally Savvy Christian*, Dick Staub accurately describes

---

2. Note to possibly offended readers: My publisher is concerned that the words "stripper" and "crap" will be offensive to some readers, so I will briefly address this concern. Many Christians find certain buzzwords offensive, which, I believe, is detrimental to our being salt and light in the world. If you're offended by the word "stripper," what happens if you actually meet someone who has made the unfortunate career choice of stripping? Do you think she (or he) might sense your immediate but unspoken rejection of her (or his) personhood? Do you think she (or he) would feel this same rejection from Jesus? And as for the word "crap," let's be honest: It's a very useful word.

the current state of evangelicalism: "There is ample evidence that in attempting to influence culture, Christians have jettisoned basic, historic Christian beliefs . . . How else can you describe a situation in which most church-going adults reject the accuracy of the Bible, claim that Jesus sinned, believe that good works will persuade God to forgive their sins, and describe their commitment to Christianity as moderate or even less firm? Our numbers indicate strength, but our shallowness betrays our weakness."[3]

The Church is in a most dire situation, the fundamentals are being disturbed—some guardians asleep at the gate and others too pompous to be heard. Naturally, I thought to myself, *This job calls for a comedian.*

Thor Ramsey
Still September 2007
Trapped in Undisclosed Think Tank

Note to Wife:
Forgot My Key,
Please Send Help

---

3. Dick Staub, *The Culturally Savvy Christian: A Manifesto for Deepening Faith and Enriching Popular Culture in an Age of Christianity-Lite* (San Francisco: Jossey-Bass, 2007), p. 42.

CHAPTER 1

Theology:
"The Sexual Life of a Nun"[1]

I do not wish to think, or speak, or write, with moderation . . .
I am in earnest—I will not equivocate—I will not excuse—
I will not retreat a single inch—I will be heard.[2]
WILLIAM LLOYD GARRISON

Don't expect me to begin every chapter with a quote.
THOR RAMSEY

Theology is better than sex.[3]

This statement may come as good news to nuns across America, but how does it help you and me, people who think about God and still have sex, on occasion, if you're married, have taken out the trash and somehow avoided fighting about money?

If you're skeptical of this, at least consider that sex and theology are closely related. Jesus said there's no marriage in heaven, which implies there's no sex either. So, heaven won't be a big

---

1. Peter Kreeft, *Everything You Ever Wanted to Know About Heaven but Never Dreamed of Asking* (San Francisco: Ignatius Press, 1990), p. 118. Dr. Kreeft, a Catholic theologian and philosopher, coined this phrase, making the point that nuns devote their lives to prayer and the study of God. If you have issues, take it up with him.

2. Debby Applegate, *The Most Famous Man in America: The Biography of Henry Ward Beecher* (New York: Doubleday Publishing, 2007), p. 105.

3. I wrote this entire chapter before Rob Bell ever published his book on sex and God, but he beat me to the presses. Not that it's a race. It's just disappointing when you think you have a good idea and then see it on a bumper sticker the next day. "Honk if you love Jesus"? That was mine.

adjustment for married people. (Honey, that's just a cheap joke from a satisfied man.) The point is, most of us view sex as the epitome of pleasure here on Earth (though chocolate comes close for many). Yet, the Bible tells us that people can't even imagine what is prepared for those who love God. It will be better than anything we've ever experienced in life, because we will be in the presence of perfect Love where we will explore God forever, which is, basically, theology.

Hence, theology is better than sex.

Look, I like pizza, but I don't eat it during sex. It's unnecessary. And forbidden by my wife. In the same way, in heaven, theology will be sex, and sex will only be pizza. And hopefully, in heaven, we'll have theology more than once a month.

Theology is not just thinking about God. Theology is a Presence. You think about God because this Presence is with you. That's really what Christian spirituality is—exploring the Presence of God in our lives or in the lives of others if you have the gift of being judgmental, which I do.

Here are the big questions regarding theology: Is it really boring, or do nuns know something that we don't? How certain can we be of our theological positions? Are some things in theology more important than others? Let me answer these questions with a story, since that will take less study.

My most recent theological journey began with my second conversion experience. (Like many Christians today, I have several conversion stories.) Sometimes it takes a crisis of life to bring us to our knees. Or marriage. Six months after our wedding day, I needed help. I needed someone to keep me from ruining my marriage. I had a nasty hankering to, how shall I say, eat pizza with other women. So, it was God or a therapist, and God was cheaper.

This is absolutely no reflection upon my wife, who is a wonderful woman, but more a reflection of our culture and the abundant availability of pizza. You too may have noticed this if you are male. Whenever you leave your home, scantily clad women are everywhere, especially if you happen to be using your metal detector at the beach. Since I was suffering from the biblical temptation of illicit pizza, I figured that's the God I should go to for help. Honestly, the night I prayed, "God, if You can do something with my life, it's Yours," I didn't know if I would be a Christian the next day, because I knew I couldn't keep *myself* from eating pizza. It was just a day-to-day struggle for me because I lacked all moral resolve.

I wanted to tell my wife that I intended to start attending church somewhere, specifically one that's a good distance from the beach, but found it difficult. Part two of my plan: The church attendance would be topped off with daily prayer and Bible reading, because despite opinions to the contrary, these things are still helpful. Now, I knew my wife was sympathetic to Christianity, but she was not what I would call a practicing Christian, the evidence for this being that no practicing Christian would have married me.

Of all places, at a Pizza Hut somewhere in the middle of a string of comedy gigs, I sat with my wife, wanting to tell her of my desire to follow Christ but unable to do so. My mouth would open and nothing would come out, making me feel like Charlton Heston in *Planet of the Apes*. Poor Bright Eyes. I prayed silently for help, which is how I suggest praying in restaurants. Otherwise, you spook the waitress. Moments after my prayer, my wife says, "Do you have something you want to tell me?"

Now, that may not seem like a big deal to you, but that was the beginning of my theological journey, my first real answer to prayer, a faint hint that God might actually like me. After that, it was easy to tell my wife that I wanted to start following Jesus. She actually felt like it was an answer to prayer, because she hates the beach and wanted to sell my metal detector.

Soon after, I played this dingy little comedy club in the basement of an old brick building in Cedar Rapids, Iowa. Not a place you'd expect to find God, even though Iowa is chock full of cornfields with baseball parks in the middle of them haunted by the ghosts of former players and everything. Some other comic was on stage fouling up the air: "I date this girl for two years—and then the nagging starts: 'I wanna know your name.'"[4]

This was my life. Telling sophomoric jokes with other irresponsible humans (aka comedians). Each weekend, I was in a new seedy little bar doing my shtick—a word used only by my mother and other people in their 70s to describe what a comedian does. The depression overwhelmed me. I bet that more people pray in comedy clubs than we realize. (You would have if you had seen my act in those days.) While I sat in the back that night, waiting my turn to talk about sex in public, I bowed my head and talked to God in that tone you use when seeing your parents for the first time in a decade because you just didn't call for some reason. It's not time to explain your bad behavior, because they're just so incredibly happy to see you.

Well, in the middle of some seedy little bar in Cedar Rapids, Iowa, I sensed God's kindness toward me, this invisible hand guiding me toward a brighter future. Maybe it was just the spotlight, but I'm pretty sure it was God. There was Jesus, hanging out with pagans, whores, lepers and comedians again.[5] I didn't expect it, and neither did the club manager. But that's what happens when a comedian thinks about Jesus. The bartenders notice the difference right away. "Liquor sales are down. But oddly

---

4. Comedian Mike Binder, who is now a big-time director.

5. I owe the phrase "pagans, whores and lepers" to John Fischer. I added the "comedians" part, because I figure that since we're at the bottom of the showbiz food chain, we might as well be added to the list.

enough, wine sales are up. And we can't keep the breadsticks in stock."

God as a Presence is very surprising, much like a Living theology. You can't rein in theology anymore than you can restrain God and strap Him in a car seat. You can wrap Him in swaddling clothes, but that's where theology comes alive—God incarnate. Theology is alive and moving and dripping with the sweat of better brows. Although they are mostly the unplucked brows of elderly professors with runaway hairs, they are better brows just the same.

There's an old joke that floats from comic to comic in the hours after the shows. The truism is basically told over a Grand Slam breakfast, after last call and numerous rejections by Hairspray Industry Supporters from small towns who can't dance but still insist on doing it in groups. One of the comedic sages points out a really beautiful lady to his cohort and chimes, "For every beautiful chick you see, there's some dude who's tired of sleeping with her." It is usually stated more crudely, of course, and it's a sad thought on many levels, to be sure, but the basic sentiment is that even sex with the most beautiful woman in the world gets boring eventually.

Theology will not disappoint you.

Theology is alive.

Even Charles Finney, controversial theologian of the Second Great Awakening and founding president of Oberlin College,[6] wrote in the preface to his *Systematic Theology*, "The discovery of new truth will modify old views and opinions, and there is perhaps no end to this process with finite minds in any world."[7]

Theology will always surprise us.

---

6. I'll be name-dropping various colleges throughout, hoping one will appreciate the plug and give me an honorary doctorate.

7. I just wish Finney's theology had been modified before he died. I love Finney but abhor his errors.

But does this mean that Truth is ever changing?

Truth is not based on personal preference, but upon, well, whoever decides what Truth is from the beginning of time. That would be God, by the way. It's a small-group leader's responsibility to discover that Truth and make it as confusing as possible when explaining it. This is why your pastor is so important. Your small-group leader could be nuts. Then again, your pastor might be nuts, too, and that's why it's always important to evaluate everyone's teaching in light of the Bible. Theology always surprises us because our understanding of Truth becomes clearer and deeper over time. Our lives should conform more closely to the Truth as we study the Bible and pray about what we're studying, experiencing God in the process.

Some of you may believe that you cannot discover Truth. If this is true, you have actually discovered a truth. You might as well continue searching for more. And it's not that you just find Truth and you're done. That's such a shallow view of Truth. As you grow spiritually—assuming that you have a soul—you will gain a better understanding of Truth. Our goal as people should be to become truer people; the outside of us getting closer to what's actually on the inside of us; living lives of complete authenticity (unless you're dating—then you're just trying to trick someone into thinking you're wonderful).

This idea of becoming the truest person that you can be is only possible if you're following the Truth. Christ is the Truth—the word of God in the flesh. And His depths we will never fully know, so theology will always be something that grows deeper and deeper as you read and study, unless you own a television. Then you can just watch Christian TV, and they'll let you know what to do.

This idea of dynamic theology will be troubling to some Christians, because many feel that the orthodox faith has been delivered in final form and that the job of the church is to regurgitate the Bible rather than explore it and discover it more fully. And if you've been to church lately, you know that Jesus probably isn't so pleased with some of our regurgitation. Even Jesus mentions the fact that He might regurgitate some of our churches out of His mouth (see Rev. 3:16). So, if you've ever witnessed the type of religious behavior from a Christian that makes you want to puke, Jesus knows just how you feel.

Struggling to understand the dogma of the Bible and the life of Christ has gone on for centuries, mostly without humor. Disregarding the Early Church fathers is really foolish. We can learn from them and gain a better understanding of what it has always meant to be a Christian. For instance, it took the Early Church several centuries to come to terms with the Trinity. Thanks to their work, it should only take you a few days. Just because we're standing on the shoulders of the Early Church fathers doesn't mean we don't have to search things out. Besides, people were shorter back then.

When it comes to Christian theology, you may not be absolutely certain about your doctrines—unless you're Reformed—but you can be certain enough. We may have difficulty narrowing down our theological positions with an arrogant certitude, but we can be certain of what the Bible does not teach regarding redemption. That's why it's good to dialogue about the important things in theology—the essential things, the things that only surprise us because they're so clear.

The great theologian H. Richard Niebuhr once said, "Laughter is the beginning of prayer." I find this concept intriguing, because I thought guilt was the beginning of prayer. If laughter is the beginning of prayer, then the greatest punch line in all of history is the resurrection of Christ. There has never been a greater surprise than a Man conquering death.

Sad faces on the road to Emmaus, "They crucified him" (Luke 24:20).

"I'm alive again—tah dah!"

Jesus *is* magic.

Theology is just thinking about God after He has done something in our lives or after you've received mercy upon mercy and promised never to do that again in hopes that the IRS won't fine you this time. When you find yourself moving and living and aware of your existence in God, you often think about why things worked out the way they did; why the kindness God showed you led somewhere.

That's theology.

This conversation about theology has been exciting, assuming that you talk back to books like I do, but I have to go now.

It's pizza night.

CHAPTER 2

The Bible Is More Than Just a Place to Stash Your Drugs

(The Theology of "This I Know")

The life of a comedian is spent mostly in hotel rooms, airplanes and eating Buffalo wings at Applebee's, the place you go for wings after you repent. Here is something you need to understand about comedians and hotel rooms: Different comedians appear at the same club for weeklong stints, so the club uses the same hotel for every performer. In most cases, the hotel reserves the same room for every comic. Sometimes they even change the sheets. So, when one comedian leaves, another is soon there to take his place, much like a virus that keeps coming back.

In every hotel room nightstand in America there is placed a Gideon Bible, as part of our silent conspiracy to spread homophobia and sexism. (Lately, I've noticed the Book of Mormon making inroads to hotel nightstands. When Christians stay in hotel rooms, many throw the Book of Mormon in the trash. Consider it a ministry opportunity.)

One road trip, I forgot my Bible and was relieved that the Gideons make a habit of forcing their beliefs into Marriotts across the country. I pulled open the drawer of my bedside table, and sure enough, there was the Gideon Bible right next to the phone book just waiting to scare the pants off some atheist. But when I opened it, I discovered the center of every page was missing, which may explain why some Christians seem so shallow.[1] Someone had carved out a chamber the size of a deck of cards to hide pot. Some comedian before me had used the Gideon Bible to hide his drugs, thinking, "No one will ever look there. Who actually *reads* the Bible? Certainly not a cop. That would probably violate some sort of separation of church and state."

Most people hide things in places they figure that no one will ever look. That's how this road comic viewed the Bible, as irrelevant. Many people today not only see the Bible as irrelevant, but they also see it as a tome that promotes hatred and homophobia, sexism and violence and, of most concern, names like Nimrod and Dorcas.

In another hotel room, someone left a handwritten note on the inside cover of a Gideon Bible. I'll quote it exactly, spelling and all: "Important notice. This book is a work of fiction. It was written by ignorant goat-herds who by the standards of the time & geography were extremely backward compared to their contempories."[2]

Personally, I think a herd of goats writing anything is pretty advanced. What's really funny about this angry scribe is that he makes several spelling errors in two short paragraphs and then writes, "The simple scribbles contained within are turning the U.S. into a nation of morons."

Well, that's the pot calling the ketell blak.

It's no shock that wayfaring comedians mock the Bible, as that's what wayfaring does to most people. But today the undermining of the Bible is coming from God's own people, including some Emergent Church thinkers who will soon lose their status as God's own people if they keep this up. Francis Schaeffer foretold

---

1. I know, I know—I'm the one writing a theological humor book.

2. Airport Radisson, Milwaukee, Wisconsin.

this problem more than 25 years ago (which is probably why he's not so popular among the emerging crowd today), when he wrote, "Within evangelicalism there are a growing number who are modifying their views on the inerrancy of the Bible so that the full authority of Scripture is completely undercut."[3]

The Bible has miraculously transformed billions of lives, and I'm hoping this will soon include the lives of many of these emerging church leaders. My own experience with the Bible has been that it is helpful, even without the maps. (Later, I'll give a helpful overview, although I unfortunately wasn't given a budget for maps. Just be assured: You are here.) My aim isn't to demystify the Bible, but to inspire you to read it, possibly before your next stay at a hotel. That way, you can also be amazed that such a mystifying book can speak to us so clearly, just as the apostle Paul wrote: "According to the revelation of the mystery hidden for long ages past, but now revealed and made known through the prophetic writings by the command of the eternal God, so that all nations might believe and obey him" (Rom. 16:26-27). And if none of this entices you to read the Bible, then maybe my $10 million Bible-reading giveaway will. *See details below*.[4]

I understand the mindset of someone who disregards the Bible. At one time, just last week, I had the same questions as most people. Is the Bible completely without error, and if not, how does that work exactly? Where did it come from? Why do some have zippers? Years past, reading the Bible was not part of my daily routine or nightly routine or something I could quote to make people feel badly. I had to make people feel badly with nothing but my own limited vocabulary.

Now, it's one thing when the general populace devalues the Bible, but it's quite another when Christian leaders do

---

3. Francis Schaeffer, *The Great Evangelical Disaster* (*The Complete Works of Francis A. Schaeffer*, vol. 4) (Wheaton, IL: Crossway Books, 1985), p. 328.

4. Void where prohibited, which would be the chair you're sitting in.

the same. The Bible is being devalued by too many Christian leaders these days. Forty-six. I counted them, and that's too many. Read between the lines from these quotes of emerging church leaders: "The Bible is still important to us," and "The Bible is still the center for us." These are statements that have the ring of, "Just because I slept with another woman, that doesn't mean I don't love you, honey. You're still important to me."[5]

The Bible is more than important.

It's more than the center.

It's the whole kit and caboodle.[6]

But in this chapter I only have time to cover the kit.

I'll cover the caboodle in the next chapter.

Rob Bell, pastor of one of the fastest growing churches in American history, according to Hyperbole Inc., wrote, "This is part of the problem with continually insisting that one of the absolutes of the Christian faith must be a belief that 'Scripture alone' is our guide. It sounds nice, but it is not true."[7] I like Rob Bell quite a lot (one million youth leaders can't be wrong). His books are great, worth the packaging alone.

You

should

read

them

all.

---

5. The two most common reasons that pastors fall are sex and money, which is one reason I use sexual sin as a frequent example. Besides, some men actually think this way, and I'm hoping some of them will read this book.

6. It's the whole kit and caboodle of life and faith, in case you're asking, "The whole kit and caboodle of what?"

7. Rob Bell, *Velvet Elvis: Repainting the Christian Faith* (Grand Rapids, MI: Zondervan, 2006), p. 67.

However, I believe some clarifying is in order. First, if the Bible alone is not our guide *to faith and practice*, then this humor book could possibly be more influential than what is probably safe for your spiritual well-being. Rob's statement is purposefully provocative, basically implying that the Bible is not the only book we look to for information in life. When I need to look up a phone number, I don't go to the Bible. If I want to find a sample résumé, I don't turn to the book of Job.

However, by faith, the Bible is our final authority on matters of faith. That sounds silly, which is why I don't believe it. If we don't have better reasons (such as the power of the Holy Spirit doing what the Bible says He does, historical accuracy, eyewitness accounts, archaeology, prophetic foretelling and textual criticism) for believing in the authority of the Bible other than a good hunch, then feelings are really our final authority. This should be clarified, because the Church is full of people who think Gideon is just some guy who accidentally left his Bible at the hotel.

Granted, our prejudices in addition to other factors sometimes taint our interpretation of the Bible. This is why the Bible is always interpreted in the context of a community of faith. So others can tell us when we're nuts. (You're welcome.) Here's the thing though: We don't re-imagine the Bible; the Bible re-imagines us. Seeing the Light is all about the deconstruction of our hearts and minds, which comes via the words of the Bible with the Holy Spirit shining them into our hearts. Romans 10:17 says, "Faith comes from hearing the message, and the message comes through the word of Christ." This is why it's so important to find other places to stash your drugs.

The leadership of the church sets the course, and this is why ordinary Christians in some churches are taking the Bible less seriously than comedians who are only prooftexting because they have a deadline to meet. The Bible is a troubling book. We'd like some passages to just disappear because they trouble us so much, which has led to butchered translations of the Bible such as *The Good Book: The Good Parts*, a Bible translation I made up just to show you how bad things are getting.

The Bible really doesn't care if we're offended when we read it. The Bible is the Lenny Bruce of literature. People in hotels across the country are still offended by a God who would use a herd of goats to communicate His Truth.

When people speak of having a relationship with Christ, they cannot do so apart from the Bible. Trying to have a relationship with Christ apart from the Bible is like dating a shallow fashion model.[8] What's there to get to know if they don't have a mind? The Bible is a glimpse into the mind of God. And who doesn't want that? Well, besides people who are afraid of what God might think.

When I was 10 years old, my dad was experiencing serious heart problems, so I became interested in death. I asked my sister-in-law if she had a Bible. The Bible and death were obvious connections to me as a kid because people always seemed to break out a Bible when someone was stuffed in a casket.

"He's dead. What should we do with him now?"

"I dunno. Let's get out that book about death."

"Let's see. 'Ashes to ashes, dust to dust.' Oh, okay, stick him in the ground."

My sister-in-law came back with this black leather book with red-edged pages, and handed it to me. The Book had presence, baby. It was like a Little Toy Judge. The Book seemed to say, "You won't be reading me. I'll be reading you." Folks,[9] the pulpit isn't

---

8. Notice that I wrote "shallow" fashion models in order to distinguish them from the fashion models with depth. Really. No, I'm not kidding. I believe there are fashion models who think deep thoughts. Really. No, I'm not kidding.

9. Whenever I begin a sentence with "folks," this means it's going to be a meaningful and folksy saying.

for the preacher. The pulpit is for the Bible, because the Bible stands in authority above us all, even above the preacher.[10]

Well, like any book, I turned to the beginning and soon discovered this was not a good place for a 10-year-old kid to start reading the Bible, especially the *King James Version*. I read, oh, maybe three paragraphs before I closed the book, thinking to myself, *Death is hard.*

There is a saying in the comedy club world that death is easy, comedy is hard. But I'm guessing they never read a *King James* Bible. That Book can scare the comedy right out of you. (It's recommended that comedians use the *New International Version*.)

My next experience with the Bible was during a Sunday School class that my mother volunteered to teach, because the main qualification for teaching Sunday School at this particular church was not being incarcerated.

"I'm on parole."

"Good, as long as you scare the children. We just don't want them damaging any more church property."

Look, I love my mother, but since becoming a follower of Jesus as an adult, I can honestly look back and say that we were not a Christian family, as evidenced by my dad shooting the neighbor's dog for barking. That's not to say I didn't have a wonderful childhood. I had a great childhood, very peaceful and quiet, certainly devoid of barking dogs.

My mother taught Sunday School during a period of my life when my parents had a slight concern for my moral education. And don't think it unkind of me to say "slight concern," because this is the kind of value system my mother taught me as a kid: "Once you tell a lie, you'd better stick to it." Of course, now we teach our daughter, "Don't believe a word your grandma says."

---

10. I think I heard Mark Driscoll say this. I think. If not, then it was me.

For Sunday School, my mother had us read from the book of Genesis in the *King James Version*. Then we were supposed to discuss what we read; but after three verses, two of the children had aneurisms, so we went straight to crafts.

There were some things we enjoyed about the Bible. We enjoyed making fun of the Elizabethan English, especially the talking snake that spoke in Elizabethan English. This class full of prideful nine-year-old Sam Harris-like skeptics bombarded my poor mother: "Lady, are you trying to tell me I'm supposed to believe we all came from just two people?"

My mother thoughtfully tilted her head and then said something I will never soon forget: "How would you like to make a paperweight with your picture in it?"

Thus concluded my childhood Bible training.

I never picked up another Bible until I was a freshman in college. The translation of the Bible I was given by a college roommate was the *Living Bible*, a paraphrased version that is one step away from having cartoons. I read the entire New Testament in a week, aside from Revelation, because that's tough in any translation; but it's a great book to read aloud to your girlfriend when you want her to break up with you.

"She has become a home for demons and a haunt for every evil spirit, a haunt for every unclean and detestable bird for . . ." (Rev. 18:2).

"I don't think we should see each other anymore."

Still, there's only one thing wrong with reading the Bible, and that's if you never do anything it says. This is the physical part of the relationship. Look, I love my wife for her mind, but if she was only a brain in a glass jar, I probably wouldn't have dated her. Relationships are both mental and physical. Translation: If you don't get to touch them eventually, you go nuts.

In high school, I used to go to this local department store called Younkers, pick out a bunch of clothing, disappear into the dressing room and strip down to steal it. One piece over the other, shirts over shirts and pants over pants, I'd put on the clothing, put the clothes I wore in over them, then walk out of the store breaking every rule ever recited on *What Not to Wear*. I'm pretty sure this is not what they mean by layering. Alas, this is why clothing now has tags on it that beep when you walk out, because of idiots like me.

After I became a Christian in college, I read a story in the Gospel of Luke about this man name Zacchaeus, a rich tax collector who gouged and cheated the people. Today, we would call him the government. *Ba-da-bing*. When he met Jesus, he stood up and said to the Lord, "Look, Lord! Here and now I give half of my possessions to the poor, and if I have cheated anybody out of anything, I will pay back four times the amount" (Luke 19:8). This story really spoke to me because I used to walk out of Younkers with four times the clothing.

That next summer after my first year of college, I went to Younkers department store and timidly asked a customer service person, "Who should I speak to about paying for some clothing that I stole last year, and might I please purchase a new pair of pants right now since I just peed the ones I am wearing?" A few minutes later this nice lady showed me into the office of the department store's principal. I didn't even know department stores had principals, but I just kept repeating to myself, "He's called a princi*pal* because he's my pal."

He asked me to explain what I was doing. Again. *Didn't that lady tell you?*

In the quietest voice I've ever spoken with in my life, I said, "I used to come here regularly and steal clothing, but I became a Christian last year, so I'd like to pay for what I took. I don't know the exact amount, but I've estimated it."

Then I placed a check on his desk that assumed each article of clothing was made for under a nickel.

He took the check and looked it over.

"This is very unusual," he said. "Tell me about what happened to you."

Now, this is where I should have a great story about how I boldly shared my experience of coming to Christ, and then prayed with this department store executive to accept Christ right there in his office; but I was tired of sitting in the stew of my own peed pants and just wanted to get out of there as fast I as could.

But he was pretty persistent in his questioning.

I verbalized what happened to me as best I could, something along the lines of, "I went to college. I was bad. I accepted Jesus." It was pretty compelling apologetics.

The only way to get to know the mind of Christ is by reading the Bible, and the only way to display our affection for Jesus is by implementing what the Bible says, even if it means that sometimes you have to wet your pants. Sometimes it's not so hard to understand what the Bible wants us to do, but for some reason, we have a hard time doing it. At other times, the Bible can be hard to understand. That is why I have written a helpful overview (without the aid of a net).

The word "Bible" comes from the Greek word *biblia*, and it means "books." The Bible actually contains 66 books, but they're all published together in one volume because the Bible was written before marketing was invented.

The Bible is split into two sections: the Old Testament, which is the Jewish section, and the New Testament, which is the Blame the Jews section. (*Hopefully, you understand irony, but one can never be too sure in the hypersensitive culture of today, so let me just state unequivocally: I am being ironic about blaming the Jews.*) It's amazing to me that Christians ever blamed the Jews for killing Jesus. I thought Jesus' death was a good thing. I mean, before I became a Christian, my college roommate was always telling me that Jesus died for my sins. The way he said it, I knew that it was supposed to make me happy. He might as well have said, "The Jews killed Jesus for your sins." Jesus being killed on a cross was a good thing for us, according to Christian theology, because it was there that He bore our sins. Theologically, His death and resurrection is what makes my life meaningful.[11] So, if you happen to be Jewish, and you're reading this, then thank you. Thank you, because I needed a Savior. Thank you for Mary and Joseph and John and Paul and Matthew and James and Peter and all the other Jews who made my faith possible by writing the Bible.

That's right—Jews wrote most of the Bible (both halves).

Christianity *is* Jewish.

If it wasn't for the Jews, there would be no Gideons.

Jewish believers wrote most of the New Testament and all of the Old Testament. The first followers of Jesus were Jewish because Jesus was Jewish. It's really a Jewish thing. It even says in the New Testament that we're all children of Abraham by faith, which basically means that I'm Jewish. That's right, by becoming a follower of Jesus, I became Jewish. You might want to pass that along to the Klan or the Kokomo Chamber of Commerce or whatever it's called these days. *Take off the sheets, boys. You're Jewish.* Now, that's tolerance when you can take a Klansman and make him Jewish.

The apostle Paul, a Jewish guy, wrote in the book of Galatians, "Consider Abraham: 'He believed God and it was credited to him as righteousness.' Understand, then, that those who believe are children of Abraham" (3:6-7).

---

11. This isn't to say that the life of Christ alone wouldn't have had a major historical impact. His miracles and teachings alone may have survived, but the fact that He continues to interact with His followers today really moves things along. His death and resurrection are still the two instances that make everything else He said and did ultimately meaningful. It's what separates Christ from every other guru and teacher. It's kind of like, "God loves Buddha, but Jesus died for your sins." It's going to be more helpful in the long run.

There.

I believe.

That makes me Jewish.

It's an important distinction to me, because my grandfather was a member of the Nazi party. Oddly enough, my grandmother was the pro-Hitler enthusiast of the family while my grandfather was a Nazi out of spineless necessity. He was an accountant who wanted to keep his job, so he counted money for the Nazi party, something akin to an IRS agent with a spiked helmet.

He was simply an accountant who looked like a biker.

Later in the war, my granddad did obtain some false documents to help an inter-religious married couple—one German, one Jewish—escape to America. This is what I am told by my mother, anyway. Whenever my mother tells me stories of her childhood, it's like *The Sound of Music* from the wrong side of the tracks. Instead of the Von Trapp family, it's the family trapped by the Vons, a pro-Hitler German family with a bunch of nosy kids. It's only heartwarming and inspiring if you're a skinhead with a swastika tattooed on your forehead.

My grandfather hid my mother, her sister and my grandmother at a Catholic nunnery until the war was over. This is the same convent that my uncle hid away in after deserting the Nazi party during the war, which is the one thing I can be proud of—we have a deserter in the family.

Naturally, I'm ashamed of my heritage, which I suppose is why I became a stand-up comedian. My philosophy of life is pretty much—make a Jew laugh. Whatever people say about me, I want them to at least say, "Thor Ramsey makes Jews laugh." Because that's not something you often hear said of Germans: "He's one funny Nazi sonuvagun."

So you can see why the Hebrew Bible has always been important to me.

The idea behind Christianity being Jewish is that God called the nation of Israel. God invented the Jewish nation. He called one man, Abraham—well, he probably called several, but Abraham was the only one who didn't wet his pants. Then God built an entire nation from that one man, which makes you wonder why there are no malls dedicated to him. It was through the Jewish nation that God chose to send His Son, who was a fulfillment of Jewish prophecies.[12] He came as a Jew through the Jewish nation to embrace all people who are willing to be embraced, but Jews first. If there is such a thing as spiritual etiquette, it is that—Jews first.

The Old Testament was written a long, long time ago, thus its fitting name. It wasn't written down initially. It was passed on orally, but the Israelites wrote it down after a nasty canker sore outbreak. Tradition says that Moses wrote the first five books of the Bible, but due to insufficient evidence, we don't really know what kind of advance he received. The books may have been ghostwritten—*yeah, Holy Ghost-written. Can I get an Amen?*

The history of the Jews in the Old Testament is wrapped in theology, much like a spiritual burrito, the tortilla being the history of the Jews and the tasty center being God's interactions with them. The problem with these ancient stories is that they have both supernatural and historical elements. The supernatural parts have prejudiced some scholars who find Mexican food too spicy. This is a theme you will find throughout modern biblical scholarship: Miracles are spicy.

Scribes then copied the writings down year after year, but this doesn't diminish their reliability. The chief scribe was a

---

12. The Jewish part of the Bible was written 1,400 years or more before Jesus was ever born and, personally, I find these prophecies very compelling. So, if you're the type who needs evidential claims, by all means, dig into some of these passages (beware your open-mindedness though—that's how I became a Christian): Jeremiah 23:5, Micah 5:2, Isaiah 61:1-2, Isaiah 53:2-6, Psalm 22:15-18. There are bunches more, but this isn't that kind of book.

monk named Xerox and, though very careful, he was known for running out of ink. Journalist Jeffery Sheler in his book *Is the Bible True?* clarifies this point: "As one scholar has noted, the stern injunction of the Bible itself in Deuteronomy 4:2 that 'you must neither add anything to the word which I command you, nor take away from it,' likely would have served to restrain most scribes from engaging in 'creative editing.'"[13]

If you happen to be a secretary and your boss says, "Take a letter. And if you misquote me, you're gonna die of staple wounds to the head," you'll probably take a pretty good letter. These were not scribe hobbyists or even goats with pens. They believed it was a message from God, more so than the Blues Brothers.

While Orthodox Jews believe that the Old Testament (or Hebrew Bible) is inspired by God, orthodox Christians believe that both halves of the Bible are inspired by God. However, I will save the subject of inspiration for the next chapter, because I just don't feel like writing about it now.

All the books of the New Testament were written in the first century, primarily by friends of Jesus, which is why the New Testament has a decidedly pro-Jesus bias. These letters circulated throughout the churches, but then this guy named Marcion[14] (not to be confused with the cheesy noodles) had some crazy ideas, and the church leaders were like, "This guy's nuts." Thankfully, Christian television did not yet exist, so it wasn't quite so embarrassing for the Church to have a lunatic running around. Still, there were various false letters circulating, written by Gnostics (a sect known for refusing to pronounce the letter "g") and other sects that were warping the

---

13. Jeffery L. Sheler, *Is the Bible True? How Modern Debates and Discoveries Affirm the Essence of the Scriptures* (New York: HarperCollins Publishers, Inc., 2000), p. 17.

14. Marcion believed that the God of the Old Testament was distinct from the God of the New Testament. In other words, they were two different gods. He didn't understand that Christianity is Jewish.

truth, so the Church leaders thought it would be wise to make the good books that were circulating official. And that's why the Bible is sometimes referred to as the Good Book—because it wasn't written by a guy who was nuts.

After the New Testament books were made official, about 400 years after the birth of Jesus, everyone in ministry was given a really nice robe, and soon the Church became lazy; but what do you expect when you spend all day lounging around in a robe? The Church of Lazy neglected to practice some really good ideas that Jesus propagated, like loving your neighbor as yourself and not giving false witness. The neglect of these ideas is known as the Crusades and the Inquisition.

The New Testament serves as a guide, letting us know what ideas about Christianity are really good and what ideas about Christianity are really bad. For instance, we understand from the New Testament that leaving behind all your material possessions to work among the poor in a foreign land or the inner city of Philly is a good idea, while promising people that God will make them rich if they give to your ministry . . . not so much.

Discovering the meaning of a text is called exegesis (bless you) and this is really important; otherwise, you end up with the Crusades. You need to understand what the original author actually meant so that you won't go around saying silly things like "the apostles were wealthy."[15] To understand what the original authors meant, it helps to have lived 2,000 years ago. Barring this, a good translation helps.

Interpretation is trickier than most of us care to admit. Many evangelicals still believe "that everyone who reads the

---

15. I actually heard a TV preacher by the name of Dr. Price spout this idea. It's funny to me how many of these prosperity preachers have names like Price and Dollar. Apparently, they are unfamiliar with the concept of irony.

Bible without prejudice will see things exactly as we do. The Holy Spirit will make sure of it."[16] Of course, this view doesn't take into account that we are idiots. We get things wrong all the time. Sure, the Bible is hard to understand, but we can understand it enough. That was Mark Twain's point: "It ain't those parts of the Bible that I can't understand that bother me—it's the parts that I do understand." (I just received an award for being the one-millionth person to quote Twain while writing in defense of the Bible. Let it be duly noted that Twain wrote some really horrible things about God and the Bible. This was just Twain on a good day for Christians. Twain, in fact, hated religion, and especially Christianity. Still, I'll quote him when it suits my purposes, just like everybody else.)

Interpretation is not the idea that you can make the Bible say anything you want, which I hear idiots say all the time, but it's finding those things the Bible is saying more clearly than others. And calling people idiots is very biblical because in the book of Ecclesiastes, Solomon wrote, "So I turned my mind to understand, to investigate and to search out wisdom and the scheme of things and to understand the stupidity of wickedness and the madness of folly." Basically, sin makes you stupid.[17] The more you sin, the dumber you become, until finally, you're an idiot. And that's how you end up with 800 wives just like Solomon. It always pays to follow your own advice.

I have had the same questions as most people about applying the Bible to life, but the big question is (because I have used size 20-point font):

Should we take the Bible literally?

16. Jon M. Sweeney, *Born Again and Again: Surprising Gifts of a Fundamentalist Childhood* (Brewster, MA: Paraclete Press, 2005), p. 16.

17. John Wimber said this, but he was quoting a friend (I think). Apparently, because of sin, I'm too stupid to remember.

Throughout the history of the Bible, scholars would come along and say, "It's religious propaganda. David is a mythological character." Then someone would discover an archaeological inscription that mentions King David. Then some scholars would say, "Well, Nebuchadnezzar never existed. There's no proof outside of the Bible itself." Then archaeologists discovered Nebuchadnezzar's palace and other ruins with inscriptions. Then they discovered King Sargon, another "figure whose existence was doubted."[18] So, I guess the one thing you shouldn't take literally is the word of biblical scholars.

Still, some preachers are just as afraid of the Bible as the people who find the Bible in hotel rooms dangerous. When your pastor, assuming that you attend church, says he's going to be teaching through the Bible, I can guarantee you he's going to skip some parts. He's probably going to skip the part about Onan spilling his seed on the ground whenever he lay with his brother's wife (see Gen. 38:9), and other similar passages.

Apparently, the Bible is not as family friendly as we've been led to believe.

The Bible doesn't do what we often do in the Christian community—sweep the dirt under the rug or at least under an embarrassing evangelist's hairpiece. We usually omit the messy parts about historic revivals and Church history and Old Testament genocide and all the parts where Jesus talks about hell. The Bible is not concerned with making God's people look good. It doesn't spoon-feed anyone who reads it. It's not afraid of you not getting it.

Even the apostle Peter, Jesus' main apostle, said Paul's letters "contain some things that are hard to understand" (2 Pet. 3:16). The Bible is concerned about telling the truth of the matter; and if you've ever had the truth of the matter told about

---

18. Sheler, *Is the Bible True?* p. 22.

you, you will readily admit the truth is not flattering, especially if there's an evangelist and a hairpiece involved.

Most important, the Bible was written to tell the truth about Jesus. This is why the writers of the four Gospels are still the most popular foursome in history, outranking even the Beatles who placed second, followed by Notre Dame's 1924 Four Horsemen backfield who "rank a distant third."[19] (The Monkees didn't make the list.) All the books of the Bible point to Jesus. The Old Testament points to what's going to happen 400 years after the book of Malachi is written, which is the coming of Messiah, and the New Testament points back to the Old Testament, saying, "See? They told you everything that was going to happen concerning Him." The two books point back and forth at each other, and together they point straight at Jesus. The Old Testament predicts the coming Messiah before the destruction of the Temple in A.D. 70, and the New Testament records what happened after the Messiah came to earth.[20] In summary, you can't diminish the Bible without diminishing Jesus.

Still, if you happen to be offended by the Gideon Bibles placed in hotel rooms across the country, just remember, you can always throw the Book of Mormon away.

Sleep tight.

---

19. Chuck Klosterman, *Chuck Klosterman IV: A Decade of Curious People and Dangerous Ideas* (New York: Scribner, 2007), p. 205.

20. These ideas came from a Mark Driscoll talk on the Bible.

CHAPTER 3

THIS CHAPTER IS PRESENTED TO:

_____

by

_____

on

(The Theology of Inspiration vs. Perspiration)

The vast majority of evangelical Christians believe what the apostle Paul expresses so beautifully: "All scripture is inspired by God and is useful for teaching, for reproof, for correction, and for training in righteousness" (2 Tim. 3:16). In other words, when you tell someone off, quote the Bible. The reason that Christians are so often telling people off is because they believe that the Bible speaks authoritatively to all people in all cultures, especially if you're gay or lesbian.

People are asking questions about the Bible and its inspiration. I don't know who they are or why they're standing outside my bedroom window yelling, but they're asking, (1) If the words of the Bible are "living and active" and are able to expose the "thoughts and intentions of your heart," do you even need to believe it for it to begin its transformative process on you? Is reading the Bible aloud to your mother-in-law seven nights a week too much? And (2) Can quoting the Bible unwisely do more harm than good? (Next time you get pulled over for speeding, quote this Bible verse to the officer, "The unclean spirits entered the pigs" (Mark 5:13), and see if things don't go worse for you from then on.)

There is much confusion about the doctrine of biblical inspiration, most of it arising from the fact that after the title "Bible," it doesn't say "by God." People wonder how God could supernaturally direct people to write accurately about eternal truth.

It's vital that we determine whether or not the Bible is inspired by God, because it's the only thing that keeps many of us from flipping the bird at blinker-less motorists. The Bible is where we get our theology. Inspiration is where we get our authority to tell people they're nuts. Good theologians distinguish between the revealed Word of God (the Bible) and our theology, which is our interpretation of the revealed Word of God. Simply stated, there's always the possibility that Calvinists could be wrong. You see, religion is just explaining what God has graciously revealed, to the best of our understanding or to the best of someone else's understanding, like John Calvin.[1] In other words, as far as we or John Calvin can tell, this is what the Bible is saying about sin or redemption or men wearing Easter bonnets, even though Eddie Izzard pulls it off nicely.

Let's be clear on this point, though. God didn't write the Bible, He inspired it, and there's a big difference, namely third-person instead of first-person narrative. The Bible says, "In the beginning, God created . . ." not "In the beginning, I created . . ."

God let other people write the Bible with their own words, personalities, limited knowledge of the world and lack of competent secretarial pools to choose from. But God, through His Holy Spirit, communicated the Truth He wanted us to know

---

1. If you don't know who John Calvin is, I cover that in chapter 14; but since I've become a Calvinist empathizer, I have dropped the chapter. However, you can view the dropped chapter on the blog www.comediansguidetotheology.com.

through these people. And this presents us with another key question: (4) If the Holy Spirit lives in you, does that mean you're Bono?

The Bible teaches that it is inspired, but this is not a good place to begin with the doctrine of inspiration. Saying that the Bible is the Word of God because it says so is called circular reasoning. It's kind of like saying your husband is very intelligent because he married you. He has the IQ of a rutabaga, but when it comes to marriage . . . he's a genius.[2]

Some Emergent Church leaders are undermining the inspiration of the Bible by undermining the reliability of words in general. Former mega-church pastor Spencer Burke wrote, "Words—even in the Bible—are fluid and unstable, and their meanings shift and change."[3] If we cannot figure out the meaning of words, if words are really ever changing, then we are up a chit sreek pithout a waddle.

This is going to be a dangerous statement, ripe for misunderstanding, but I believe that the Bible is true whether God inspired it or not. Now, what I mean by that is, I believe that the stories in the Bible actually happened. I believe that God interacted with Abraham, Isaac, Jacob, Joseph, Moses, and all the rest. I believe that the authors of the Bible accurately wrote these stories, unlike the publishers of most children's Bibles. (They always cover Jonah and the big fish, but never Job and the pus boils. Look, if you tell a child the story of Noah and the ark, but you leave out the part about why he had to build an ark to begin with, it's really just a story about animals on a rainy day. You might as well reduce the story of Jesus to a guy who carries around sheep.)

Now, if God breathed a special blessing on their pens as they were writing the stories, thankfully, they held the papyrus

---

2. This joke can also be applied to wives.

3. Spencer Burke and Barry Taylor, *A Heretic's Guide to Eternity* (San Francisco: Jossey-Bass, 2006), somewhere near the middle of the book.

down with their other hand so it wouldn't blow away. The point is, if the stories are true, then we're actually in the same boat as if the Bible was written by God anyway, because God wrote the stories of these lives.

Bible translator J. B. Phillips wrote, in his little book *The Ring of Truth*, that "any man who has sense as well as faith is bound to conclude that it is the *truths* which are inspired and not the words which are merely the vehicles of truth."[4]

That's inspiration.

It's the words of man—plus.

Inspiration *plus* perspiration.

Some scholars call this dual authorship.

In this respect, the Bible is just like Jesus, fully human and fully God.

"Above all, you must understand that no prophecy of Scripture came about by the prophet's own interpretation. For prophecy never had its origin in the will of man, but men spoke from God as they were carried along by the Holy Spirit" (2 Pet. 1:20-21).

It's the words of man conveying the thoughts of God, which are troubling enough. God would tell the prophets and the prophets would tell the people, sometimes without much clothing on (see Isa. 20:3), which was really troubling or at least distracting. But there is plenty of evidence that people don't want God speaking directly to them. For example, when God spoke aloud to the nation of Israel, they all complained to Moses because it frightened them, "That's enough of that. We don't have that much fresh underwear."

We often don't really want to hear from God, and many times we struggle with accepting even the simplest truths from the Bible. Whenever you tell someone that you believe that

---

4. J. B. Phillips, *Ring of Truth: A Translator's Testimony* (Vancouver, BC: Regent College Publishing, 2004), p. 29.

the Bible is God's Word, they often look at you funny. So I've determined that this is no way to begin a conversation with the convenience store clerk. Just take your beer and go home.

If you don't want to be embarrassed publicly by talking about the Bible, you can always give the Bible a nickname like "The Best Kept Secret of My Life" or "Shirley." But when you tell people that you found Shirley hard to understand until you purchased *Nelson's Illustrated Shirley Dictionary*, they still look at you funny. Just take your beer and go home.

For a while, I called the Bible "the Scriptures" because it sounded more mature and intelligent. "The Bible" just sounded so "B-i-b-l-e, yes that's the book for me." It sounded so Sunday School. It just had negative connotations to me, like Bible-thumper. I'm against thumping in general, let alone with a Bible. Sometimes I'll call the Bible "the Biblioteque." That's kind of a cool French word. (Biblioteque is a place where people who believe in the Bible go to dance.)

Though I don't want to be known as a Bible-thumper, sometimes there's no getting around it. Some people just need a good whack on the head. Actually, I am never what I consider to be obnoxious about my faith in the comedy clubs whenever fellow comedians might ask, "What's up with you these days?" My answer will be along the lines, "I've undergone a kind of spiritual renewal." If they want to know more, they ask. Mostly, they just think I became a vegetarian.

Sometimes they demand to know the answer to some weighty spiritual question, assuming that if you claim to have a relationship with God then suddenly you're omniscient too. Usually, I want to say, "Why don't you read the Bible for yourself?" But somehow this suggestion is offensive to a guy doing shots of Tequila.

Sometimes they're coherent enough to ask, "How can you think the Bible's the Word of God?" Then I offer them a mint, because coherent or not, Tequila makes your breath stink.

In the early nineties, after I experienced God in a Pizza Hut (as detailed in chapter 1), I made a commitment to God to read the Bible and to pray for five minutes a day. That was a package deal, by the way. If it took me three minutes to read a chapter, then I had two minutes left to pray. (I didn't say it was a deep commitment.) Quite honestly, I didn't even know if I could maintain such a shallow commitment as this. I knew that I didn't have the moral resolve to be a good person. I still had a Cub Scout den master with a restraining order against me from when I was 10. And I certainly didn't have the wardrobe, not one "body piercing saved my life" T-shirt in my closet. I spoke plainly to God, "If You don't do it, it can't be done." Basically, as long as I'm not responsible, we have a deal.[5]

So, the first day of my tentative Christian spiritual journey, I turned to the Gospel of John, the fourth book in the New Testament, because this is where new believers, or old believers who have fallen by the wayside, are told they should begin.[6] Things were iffy enough with me already, so I certainly wasn't going to mess with protocol. I opened my dusty Bible to the Gospel of John, turned my head and coughed—it had been some time since I had cracked open a Bible, so I wasn't about to stop just because I was in the middle of my yearly physical.

There's a story in the first chapter of the Gospel of John where Jesus meets Nathaniel, a story I would like to quote for you now from *The Seinfeld Study Bible*:[7]

Int. Monk's Restaurant—Day

Philip: Hey, you're never gonna believe this!
Nate: Then don't tell me. Why get your hopes up?

---

5. I guess I'm closer to a Calvinist than I realize.

6. Postmodern Christians begin wherever they like.

7. Not an actual study Bible, so don't go embarrassing yourself at the local bookstore by asking for it by name.

Philip: I found the Messiah.

Nate: Get outta here.

Philip: Really.

Nate: Where?

Philip: Nazareth.

Nate: Nazareth? There's not a clean toilet to be found in that city.

Philip: You would know.

Nate: I would know. When I'm out, I use public toilets.

Philip: Except in Nazareth.

Nate: Except in Nazareth. They're filthy.

Philip: I found Him, I tell ya. Come see for yourself.

Nate: It's the only person I can see for.

Later . . . Philip's Apartment

Jesus: (to Nate) You're a completely honest Jew.

Nate: How do you know who I am?

Jesus: I saw you sitting under the fig tree when you were alone.

Philip: What were you doing under a fig tree?

Nate: I told you, the toilets are filthy.

Philip: You would.

Nate: (to Jesus) You saw me when I was alone? You are the Son of God and the King of Israel.

The fact that Jesus knew what Nathaniel was doing while he was alone is enough proof for Nathaniel that Jesus is the Son of God. Also, just the fact that Jesus knew what he was doing while he was alone is enough to keep many teenage boys in line. But here's where I experienced some sort of communiqué from God Himself. As I'm reading where Jesus says to Nate, "You believe because I told you I saw you under the fig tree. You shall see greater things than that," suddenly the words jumped off the page, which is something you have to watch out for when reading the Bible. If this happens to you, don't try and return the Bible. It's not defective. This just happens sometimes.

It was as if Jesus was saying to me, "You're amazed because I answered a little prayer at a Pizza Hut. I promise you that you'll see greater things than this."

This interpretation presents us with several problems: (1) No Pizza Hut in Nazareth to this day; (2) Is it really a legitimate thing to apply these words subjectively to my own life? Only if God says it's okay, which He did, so let's move on.

The situations are parallel—I hate public toilets, too. Actually, both Nathaniel and I were amazed by something small that God did, so He can say the same thing to each of us. God still uses words to get to us and He seems completely confident that His words will still make sense even when they're translated from one language to another.

That's plenty of proof for me concerning the Bible's inspiration. If you'd like something a little more weighty, I find the prophecies written by those Old Testament guys about some future Messiah pretty convincing. However, it's hard to separate a supernatural God from 300 fulfilled Old Testament prophecies. That's a lot of ground to cover, so you might want to get a snack.

Psalm 22, written 1,000 years before Jesus was crucified, states in verse 16, "They have pierced my hands and my feet." We can only conclude this to mean crucifixion, since according to most biblical scholars, tattoo parlors didn't exist at this time. Capital punishment as a means of execution wasn't invented until several hundred years later, which was good news for all the folks on death row. In this same Psalm, David also speaks of the guards throwing dice for Christ's garments.

That's 2 fulfilled prophecies, only 298 more to go.

According to one source, "Using the science of probability, we find the chances of just forty-eight of these prophecies being fulfilled in one person to be right at one in 10^{157} (a one followed by 157 zeros!),"[8] which means that somewhere in the world there is a math teacher who is a Christian.

When I begin to examine these prophecies more closely, they remind me of how Jesus used parables. They're never as clear upon first glance. And just like the parables, those who have ears to hear will hear. Those who do not will go on to teach anthropology at a small college while dismissing the Bible off-handedly to their students only later to be fired for multiple illicit affairs with undergrads. *Welcome to orientation.*

Just like Nathaniel, some of us need only small proofs to believe Jesus when He said, "Abraham rejoiced to see My day" (John 8:56). For others, even 300 fulfilled prophecies are not enough to hint at inspiration, so I'm going to stop after 2.

Still, it's not so much that the Bible is inspired as it is that Jesus rose from the dead. That's the inspiration behind the Bible, this invisible Presence that sometimes shows up when you read it. It really is living and active, and when kings and priests shut it up, terrible things can happen. The Crusaders didn't have pocket Bibles. Things might have been different if they had. Maybe one of them might have noticed that when Simon Peter cut off the ear of the high priest's servant, Jesus healed it and said, "Put your sword away." You see what a pertinent message that might have been for the Crusaders had the Bible been available to them? Where are those Gideons when you need them?

The Bible is inspired because something happened—something specific. Matthew, Mark, Luke, John and even Paul wrote about an Event, something that actually happened. They wrote

8. Josh McDowell, *A Ready Defense* (Nashville: Thomas Nelson, 1993), n.p.

about what they and others saw—Jesus Christ with grave clothes at His feet, alive again.

Tah dah!

The fact that He rose again means that He can assist you in your study of the Bible. How convenient is that! God interacts with us through the Bible, which has saved countless generations from having to change their underwear.

The way people react to the Bible is a funny thing. Some people are afraid of the possibility that the Bible is the word of God, because they're afraid of what God might have to say. Those who fear the Bible treat it one of two ways: like a bad date or like a serial killer. They ignore it or dismember it.

When I was in college, one of my good friends told me what a student at TCU wrote on the board in one of his classes. They were all taking their seats when he looked up and noticed written on the board, "Write a paper on the relevancy of the Bible. (A blank page will do.)"

The most influential book ever written is irrelevant?! Just the fact that it's the most influential book ever written makes it relevant, you silly frat boy. (Now, I have no evidence that this was written by a fraternity member, and I'd just like to state for the record that fraternities do many charitable things for their communities in addition to getting drunk at theme parties.)

Perhaps he should have asked Tatiana Goricheva about the relevance of the Bible. She was a Russian intellectual, an atheist and practitioner of yoga—which is like exercise for smart people—who wrote a little book called *Talking About God Is Dangerous*. One day while doing her exercises, using a book of yoga mantras, one of the suggested mantras was the Lord's Prayer, taken directly from the Bible. After repeating it several times while doing her yoga exercises, suddenly she just understood the gospel of Christ, and then she experienced the reality of the risen Christ right there in her living room.

The Bible is dangerous.

Apparently, yoga is not too safe either.

That's why people believe that the Bible is inspired by God—because sometimes He shows up when you read it. Sometimes He tells us He loves us, and sometimes He tells us off. But He can't tell you anything if you don't see what He has to say.

Start with a children's Bible if you must. It'll give you an overview and leave out the scary parts.

The Reality of God and the Problem of Self-Addressed Stamped Envelopes

(The Doctrine of Doubt and
How It May or May Not Help You)

For weeks I've struggled with how to begin this chapter. I don't know what I was so worried about, because I just began it right there. Not the most riveting way to stumble into our next subject, but it is a beginning. Now all I have to do is come up with a bunch of witty and insightful thoughts that will help you become the person you were meant to be, if by that you mean, a cynical grump.

Initially, I began the chapter like this:

After having a little spat with my wife, I bought some flowers. As I was about to leave the flower shop, the cashier asked, "Don't you want your receipt?"

I said, "You mean if these don't work I get my money back?"

Before she posed this simple question, I had no doubts about buying the flowers.

However, I didn't really like that chapter opening, which is why I have eliminated it. It wasn't true. I didn't have any doubts about buying flowers. I had doubts as to whether they would work or not.

After around 10 more revisions, I began the chapter like this:

Doubt can be helpful.
Just ask any couple about to get married.
I entered marriage with a certain degree of trepidation, but for one reason only. It's called wedlock.
Wed . . . lock.
There are only four words like "wedlock" that I can think of, and they are "gridlock," "headlock," "deadlock" and "hemlock."

From the get-go, I considered the above piece unsatisfactory, because people who read it kept asking, "What's hemlock?" It just wasn't working. That is why I have decided not to use it either. So, here I sit in front of my MacBook, plagued with doubt about how to begin this chapter. When suddenly it occurs to me, all this wavering is probably the best way I can begin my chapter on doubt in the Christian life, which brings us back to— "for weeks I've struggled with how to begin this chapter."

Here's what gets me. Doubt is somehow virtuous these days. People who write about doubt write about it with great certainty. They write these long theological paragraphs and then end them with, "We will never know." Man, that seems pretty certain to me. Why so certain about doubt? Why not be certain about certainty? What about the smugness of doubt?

Executive director, cofounder, innovative evangelism reinventor of Off the Map, Jim Henderson wrote in his 98-percent great little book (aside from the line I'm about to quote) called *Jim & Casper Go to Church*, "As followers of Jesus we put our faith in a set of beliefs that we choose to think of as real."[1] So, you're talking yourself into it? That's the kind of incredibly lame faith I hope my daughter makes her own as an adult. "Honey, I hope one day you also have a hunch." Unbelief is no longer a sin; it's a hunch. Actually, that's really what much of Emergent doubt is—ill-defined unbelief. Believers who actually believe are patronized, which is odd because the author of the Gospel of Luke wrote to Theophilus so that he might be certain of his faith (see Luke 1:4).

Doubt is such an epidemic in the Church that when preachers hold up the heroes of the faith as examples, they have to point to their failures to encourage us rather than their successes, because as a body of believers we can't handle their successes. They intimidate us. Even though, according to Jesus, we don't even need all that much faith to move a mountain. Yet how many times do we have to hear about David's adultery to be encouraged? To judge by most Sunday sermons, we can barely keep our pants zipped the temptation is so great . . . let alone move a mountain.

The problem with unbelief isn't an honest question from a spiritual seeker or a struggling believer; it's the persistent disbelief after plenty of evidences offered on God's behalf.[2] "Look, even if the Lord should open the floodgates of the heavens, could this happen?" (2 Kings 7:19). Many people secretly want their doubts to turn to unbelief just so they can enjoy a joint without feeling guilty.

I don't know if the following attitude is indicative of the emerging church, but I'm going to use it as an example of

---

1. Jim Henderson, Matt Casper and George Barna, *Jim and Casper Go to Church: Frank Conversations about Faith, Churches and Well-Meaning Christians* (Carol Stream, IL: Tyndale House Publishers, 2007), p. 166.

2. Paraphrased from a C. H. Spurgeon sermon called "The Sin of Unbelief." http://www.spurgeon.org/sermons/0003.htm (accessed November 2007).

the prevailing mindset just the same. Jason Boyett, who happens to be a very funny author and columnist, said to his friend, journalist Lauren Sandler, "Faith as certainty is a fascist's attitude."[3] First of all, I'm not saying to ignore your doubts or not talk about them openly as long as you're in the shower with loud music playing. Not that Jason doesn't say some helpful things about faith and doubt on his website,[4] but contrast Jason's view of certainty with how Jesus describes His disciples while praying for them: "They knew with certainty that I came from you, and they believed that you sent me" (John 17:8).

Now, Jesus isn't just talking about the lucky disciples who saw Him with dusty toes, because He goes on to say, "My prayer is not for them alone. I pray also for those who will believe in me through their message" (John 17:20). Jesus wants us to be certain of our faith in Him. If you're certain that your parents love you, there's nothing arrogant about feeling that way, just because you feel like you're their favorite. It's not like you have to tell your brothers and sisters. Besides, you'll find that they feel the same way—like they're the favorite. Most kids from functional homes are certain that "Mom and Dad love me best." Look, I doubt a lot of things about how to live as a Christian in the twenty-first century, but the one thing I am certain of is the historical resurrected Christ. But then again, maybe it's just that fascism runs in my family.

In this chapter, I will be addressing doubt with a humble degree of certitude and my fictional character Morph.

"Hi there, happy reader."

"Please, Morph, not yet."

"Sorry."

---

3. Lauren Sandler, *Righteous: Dispatches from the Evangelical Youth Movement* (New York: Viking Penguin, 2006), p. 236.

4. www.jasonboyett.com—on his downloads page you can find a talk he gave, actually a sermon, called "Faith & Doubt."

Let me introduce you now to my fictional character Morph. I call him "Morph" because he's such an Emergent Christian that he's morphed into an exact representation of popular culture at large in nearly every way, including his religious beliefs; so really, what's the point? Morph is a way for me to write creative nonfiction or what I like to call "emerging satire for people who find themselves in the story of finding things in their story."

This may sound melodramatic, especially if you crank up some Beethoven in the background, but Morph just appeared out of nowhere holding his favorite Starbucks mug (the one with the mermaid who has two tails) with a sweater tied around his shoulders because though he is an emerging church leader, he only has late-'80s fashion sense.

"So, Thor," he said to me, being in the habit of addressing me by my name, "I see that you're having some doubts about uncertainty."

"Well, I'm not saying that doubt isn't part of life for anyone's belief system, but can't we be certain about anything?"

"So, you think you can know that you know that you know that you know that you know?"

"You just spit on me."

"And one day, so will certainty. Don't be naïve. Most of us begin our Christian walks with rock-solid certainty; later, we adjust our viewpoints to deal with changing cultural shifts, or what I like to call 'personal pet sins' we'd rather not give up," said Morph, sipping his coffee, squinting and looking thoughtfully into the distance. "Why do you believe in God, Thor?"

I love when people treat the question, Why do you believe in God? like it's this tremendously complicated issue. The answer is simple: "Morph, I believe in God because I am not an idiot. Actually, that's not true. I believe in God because He has made it easy for idiots to believe in Him."

Morph nearly dropped his mug. "How has He made it easy?"

"Well, according to God, the subtle hints given in nature alone should be enough to tilt us in the direction of belief in the transcendent. As a matter of fact, Paul says there's so much proof of God in nature that when we die we'll be without excuse (see Rom. 1:20). When you look closely at nature, you will certainly see God revealed, especially if you pull back some flowers and swipe away the dirt to expose where it says, 'Made by God.'"

"Nature might hint of a Creator, but not necessarily so," Morph objects. "And even if God does exist, just because the ocean is deep doesn't mean people are. Besides, science has a different explanation for the beginning of the universe."

"Morph, as soon as science gives an explanation for how the universe began, it's stepped out of science and into theology. And if you step into theology, it's hard to get it off your shoes."

"If God exists," Morph asks, "why doesn't He just speak loudly from heaven and tell us all He's real?"

"First, you'd wreck your car. Second, insurance companies do not cover acts of God, which have no bearing on an atheist's policy, but it still makes them a little angry. Just because God stops traffic and someone becomes convinced that He is real doesn't mean they will love Him and demonstrate that love by following and obeying Him. God is looking for demonstrative lovers, not believers. The Church is full of believers and that's part of the problem. Even demons believe. So, if you only have the faith of a demon—you can get by in church."

Morph slumps away to get some Sweet-N-Low, apparently convicted by my hard-hitting, no-nonsense style, his sweater dropping on the floor behind him.

Doubt itself did not originate in hell. It originated in heaven where an angel doubted the job God was doing and was soon cast into hell where he now spends most of his time whispering to journalists about how dangerous evangelicals are.

Why do we doubt?

Hey, we all have questions:

Why can't I have two wives?

If my wife murders me, will she lose her salvation?

Who will feed the cat?

These questions are natural.

What concerns me is when writing about doubt leads to an unusually large number of indentations.

Why so many indentations?

Is the tab key broken?

We will never know.

Doubt becomes a problem when it leads to unbelief. During a recent small-group Bible study at our church, one of the participants said, "I don't believe prayer changes things." He was then taken to the pool and drowned. The one thing we did learn from this discussion was that prayers don't work under water.

We doubt simply because we are finite. As humans, our knowledge is limited, which is the only reason my wife married me. She didn't have all the information she needed. Christian spirituality is laced with mystery. True. But it's also laced with certainty.

There may be subconscious longings within the emerging church for the feeling of uncertainty. Let's be honest, the less certain we are about the Bible, the less loudly it speaks into our lives. Whereas, the more certain we are about what Jesus said, the more authority He has to speak to us in real time.

Analogy #1: The War in Iraq

Let's look at doubt, beginning with our conversion to Christ (assuming that you're converted). Using the war in Iraq, let's compare our conversion and growth process with this particular conflict. When we initially started the war in Iraq, an early victory was declared and everybody seemed happy, besides the rest of the world.

That's how it is when you first believe in Jesus. You sense the presence of the Holy Spirit who has "invaded" your soul. An early victory is declared over all your bad habits and you're oblivious to how annoying your newfound joy is to the rest of the world. Then God begins to show you the depths of your heart and the deeply rooted sin problems. Likewise, the war in Iraq is experiencing severe resistance. The enemy strongholds are much deeper than they realized. In the Christian life, when we spend our lives working through this process of defeating strongholds, it's called sanctification.[5] In the political realm, working through this resistance process is called denial.

With the war in Iraq, it probably wasn't a good idea to begin with, so the analogy really implodes here. Although as Christians, we cannot give up this fight. The insurgencies of our hearts must be overthrown. Often what happens is that you begin to doubt yourself because of the war in Iraq (your heart); and when this doubt is festering, it can lead you to doubt the GOP—in other words, God. But there is quite a distinction between doubting yourself and doubting God.

Doubting the GOP is part and parcel.

Not to brag about my expertise on doubt, but I have been given an honorary doctorate from the Doubters Institute, though I have misgivings about its authenticity. The point is, I know doubt. The story I am about to share with you is one of the most humiliating stories of my Christian life. It's a story of doubt and the miracle that followed. This story is probably why I stopped keeping a spiritual journal, other than the fact that it's hard to write on something that's ethereal. Still, why keep a record of how incredibly dumb you can be?

---

5. Alister E. McGrath, *Doubting: Growing Through the Uncertainties of Faith* (Downers Grove, IL: InterVarsity Press, 2007), p. 17.

In my possession, in a cabinet in my office, I have 30 sealed envelopes, each with an official postmark from the US Postal service. (And, no, they are not there to prove the existence of Santa Claus.) Over a decade ago, I mailed all these letters to myself so that I could one day share them with all my friends and relatives who don't believe. Yes, the contents of these letters would convince them of Christ's divinity.

Thank God for mail, huh?

My plan was to give one of these self-addressed stamped envelopes to each of my relatives. They would notice the envelope is sealed. Then they would notice the postmark: 01 JUL 1995. *What? What's this? A letter from 1995 that hasn't yet been opened?* Quickly, they would open the letter to behold the mystery inside—a full-sized bundt cake a decade old. (I only wish.) Copied on very expensive tan paper with speckles, they would find a most miraculous story, which explains my splurging for expensive paper. They would be instructed to "Look at the date of the postmark and the date it was written, and believe in miracles."

This is a painful letter to read even now, partly because of the melodramatic tone and partly because there's no bundt cake in the envelope. The only intelligent thing I wrote in this letter was, "I'm also writing because I don't have enough courage or enough faith to go around proclaiming that God will do something before He does it."

Man, was that a smart thing to do. Only share letters *after* God does a miracle. Not one second before. Otherwise, add a little Betty Crocker mix to your envelopes and hope for the best.

Okay, here's what I hoped would happen. Let me quote my former idiotic self from the actual letter. I have plenty to spare. "In December of 1994, I was staying with some relatives . . . before bed one night, reading from the Gospel of Matthew, the Lord spoke very gently to my heart while I read the following verse (8:17), 'He took our infirmities and carried our diseases.'"

I decided this meant that my wife was going to be healed and would soon get pregnant (with my dedicated assistance, of course). Well, God must have spoken extra gently because I didn't hear right. At least, I doubt that I heard right. You see where this is heading? My poor wife, suffering from collapsed fallopian tubes, wasn't healed. I told her that God told me that she would be healed, but I could tell she wasn't buying it. Standing on the kitchen table and shouting "You will be healed!" didn't seem to help either. What was her problem? It was just a matter of waiting for God to bring His promise to pass, in my mind (which is obviously unreliable). This is a tough sell to a woman in her early 30s who wants to have children. You'd think she would have avoided having children altogether considering that her husband was a lunatic.

Now, several things could have happened to my non-occurring miracle.

1. I wanted to hear from God, but didn't really.
2. I heard from God, but
   (a) doubted too much to bring about the promise by prayer
   (b) my continuous disobedience negated the promise just like the behavior of the children of Israel in the Old Testament
   (c) the moon was not in the seventh house and Jupiter did not align with Mars. Or . . .
3. I am an idiot, but God loves me anyway.

Looking back, I understand several things now that I didn't then. First, there was no need to buy expensive paper. Cheap paper would have worked just as well for a letter I didn't send telling about a miracle that never happened. Second, bill collectors complain about the cake mix and still want to know where the check is. Third, you never realize you're being an idiot when you're being one. Finally, just because God gives someone a promise is no guarantee that the promise will be fulfilled. I know that's a hard sell, but I believe there is plenty of Old Testament evidence to support such a theological claim. If you look at the children of Israel, story after story, God would make them a promise and then by their persistent rebellion—no bundt cakes.

God may love us unconditionally, but there are conditions to answered prayer. A. W. Tozer put it this way, "He (God) is not hard to please, but he may be hard to satisfy."[6]

My wife and I waited maybe six months before moving forward with in vitro fertilization because (a) if we waited and nothing happened, it would be my fault; and (b) if we waited and nothing happened, it would be my fault.

Initially, I was hesitant to share this story, not so much because it makes me out to be an idiot, but because it makes me out to be a colossal idiot. Don't get me wrong. I still believe in miracles. Nothing is impossible with God—unless there's a woman involved. Ba-da-bing. Specifically, a woman with fertility problems who wants to have a baby.

Miracles are probably more difficult in a culture of unbelief, but they're not impossible. "Let it be done to you according to your faith." Thanks for the word, Jesus, but we're going with Dr. Werlin. "Ye of little faith." You have described us perfectly. Now I have 30 envelopes asking me the question, Was I foolish or faithless?

We will never know.

"And he did not do many miracles there because of their lack of faith" (Matt. 13:58).

Well, halle-ma-lujah for the clarity of Scripture, huh?

---

6. A. W. Tozer, *The Best of A. W. Tozer,* compiled by Warren W. Wiersbe (Camp Hill, PA: Christian Publications, Inc. 1995), p. 121.

At the time, I was surely influenced by the Vineyard Movement, a church movement in which they encourage trial and error regarding miracles and all things supernatural within a Christian context. If you're not familiar with recent Church history, the Vineyard in Toronto had a controversial revival in the early nineties in which people were being slain in the Spirit (basically falling down involuntarily after someone prays for you), giving words of prophecy (God speaking to the congregation through an individual, a very controversial practice) and people roaring and barking (nowhere in the Bible). Yes, roaring and barking, like lions and dogs, something that the church leadership took a wait-and-see policy with, like the lady roaring behind me during a chorus of "Our God Is an Awesome God" could possibly be fruitful. "Our God . . . *rooooaaaar!* . . . is an awesome God . . . *grrrrroooooowwwwwllll* . . ."

Okay, simmer down there, Aslan.

The one valid point they made in all this craziness was that stranger things happened in the Bible (see 1 Sam. 19:24).

True, but that's not great church policy.

Now, I don't want to give you the impression that all Vineyard churches embraced these practices wholeheartedly. Some roared more tentatively. Some churches only meowed during worship. Eventually, the leadership of the movement took steps to correct the excesses of this revival and the Toronto Vineyard became the Toronto Formerly Vineyard. The basic Protestant move. "Church discipline? Forget you. We'll start our own church."

But I will defend the craziness of the Vineyard Churches of America, where I attended for many years, because there is a simple reason for this behavior. People who feel rejected at other churches because of their natural eccentricity or socially unacceptable status are welcomed with open arms at Vineyard Churches. They are truly a welcoming and accepting group of

people, and that's why the tares in their wheat are more noticeable than respectable congregations. They welcome "the least
of these" that some churches do not.

Plus, they have dancing flag ladies. Who doesn't love a dancing flag lady?

"So, did you abandon the miracle route?"

"Oh, hey there, Morph. Well, the answer is yes and no."

"How's that?"

"Let me tell you the rest of the story. Something I like to
call 'the rest of the story I am now telling.'"

"That's a great title. You should call this book 'The Rest of
the Story I am Now Telling.'"

"But, Morph, you're part of the story I am now telling."

"The story I find myself in?"

"Yes."

"Cool."

The fact that your background can affect your faith is
pretty universally understood. My dad died when I was 11, and
my wife's father left her family when she was about the same
age and relocated to Saudi Arabia. The point is, because we
both basically lost our fathers at a young age, neither one of us
trusts our mothers. Unfortunately, that's how life works. The
parent left behind is the one who gets blamed.

Desperate to have a family, my wife and I underwent in
vitro fertilization six times. That's why my wife still calls our
daughter a miracle baby: She got pregnant but didn't have to
sleep with me.

If you're unfamiliar with in vitro fertilization, it is a very expensive, medically innovative scientific procedure that involves
several steps. The first step is to have her dad send us a check.
Honestly, I can't thank my father-in-law enough, a mild-mannered
choir director from Michigan who made a bundle teaching the
children of American oil executives in Saudi Arabia four-part

harmonies. Thanks to dear old dad's checks, we were able to sit down with Dr. Laurence Werlin, a renowned fertility specialist who looks like a buff Einstein, wild white hair and 'stache, and ask, "Can you make us a baby?"

Dr. Werlin explained the in vitro process to us in terms most remedial biology students could understand, so naturally, we didn't really get a lot of what he had to say. The gist of it is that every egg a woman will ever release is stored in her body . . . somewhere. I don't know where. That's why it's so hard to get pregnant. Pregnancy is all about finding the egg, that much is clear. In the natural course of things, women release only one egg each month during, how shall I say . . . times of visitation. It's in Deuteronomy or something. I think. During the process of in vitro fertilization, the doctor's goal is to retrieve as many eggs as possible to fertilize and then implant them. The process of retrieving the eggs is called hyperstimulation. I only have a vague idea as to how this works. I think the doctor walks in, says "Coochie, coochie!," and then she has like 40 eggs. (Sorry to get so technical.)

The best way to explain the difference between natural pregnancy and in vitro fertilization is by looking at them like a junior high school dance.[7] (Personally, I refuse to use the term middle school. It's junior high, a junior version of senior high. It's not middle school. There are no Hobbits involved.)

Analogy #2: Natural Pregnancy as a Junior High School Dance

Okay, you have a nicely decorated gymnasium. On one side of the gym you have an eighth-grade girl. And she's a very special eighth-grade girl. She doesn't just go to dances every

---

7. I know, I know. This has somehow become the chapter of analogies.

night of the week. She only goes to that one dance once a month.

On the other side of the gym, you have two billion eighth-grade boys.

Then, the band begins to play and the boys break out in every direction, banging into the bleachers, trampling each other, fights break out, many are killed, but not one idiot makes it over to ask her to dance.

Now, that's natural pregnancy.

And by the way, all of this takes place underwater.

In vitro fertilization works like this. You have a junior high school dance. At this junior high, all of the eighth-grade girls have been taken and frozen. (Don't worry, their parents have signed permission slips.) But on the night of the dance, on one side of the gym, they place six eighth-grade girls. Again, on the other side of the gym, two billion eighth-grade boys. But you have a teacher who takes the boys by the hands, walks them over to the girls and says, "Now dance!"

And that's how babies are made.

Couples don't enjoy an in vitro pregnancy the same way as couples that get pregnant naturally, for obvious reasons. The delicate nature of the pregnancy is another reason. You don't know if you're going to be pregnant from week to week, so you don't paint the nursery or put up the crib or dream about the future. For the first trimester you have an ultrasound every week. One week there's a little heart beat on the monitor. The next week it's gone.

For two years, my wife's life consisted of nothing but shots of progesterone and bed rest. We'd been pregnant twice, the first was tubular, the second a miscarriage. Three times nothing happened. We were about to try for the sixth time when we were at a seminar where our fertility specialist, Dr. Werlin, was doing a Q&A on in vitro. Someone asked, "How many times before you tell a couple to consider other alternatives?" He said,

"Three times." My wife and I looked at each other. I whispered, "I guess we'll have to find a new doctor."

For whatever reason, burly Dr. Werlin broke his own rules, and after my wife's sixth implant, she became pregnant. These are fragile pregnancies. Dr. Werlin put her on bed rest for nearly six months this last time. I guess he wanted to make sure he was going to get all the credit. Six months of bed rest. No problemo. I'm a great coach, because I'm extremely lazy.

One night I was downstairs praying for this pregnancy and I decided to focus on God being the author of Life. I remembered there's something in the Gospel of John about Jesus and the creation of life. It says, "Without him [Christ] nothing was made. In him was life . . ." (John 1:3,4).

I prayed the Scriptures back to God, asking Him to bring life from my wife's womb. Since I was reading from the first chapter, I decided to go ahead and finish it. I turned the page and there it was—the story of Jesus and Nathaniel. I had forgotten about it. But now I am reminded, "I promise you—you shall see greater things than these." It was as if God was saying to me, "This will be one of those greater things."

I know. I know. You're skeptical because of my former track record. You see how former relationships can affect your faith? Here's the good part. My brother-in-law, Brian, this Calvary Chapel guy who is also a follower of Jesus, called my wife the next day and said, "Hey, you're not going to believe this, but last night God woke me up."

Now, you have to understand, for my brother-in-law to say that God spoke to him is outside of his normal vocabulary. He's not one of those Christians who walks around saying, "God said this to me" or "God said that to me." He doesn't bark or roar. He's extremely conservative, influenced by fine Bible teachers who believe that miracles have passed away. They're called dispensationalists, because they believe that God no longer dispenses sensational miracles. They believe that miracles were used only to give the Early Church a nice kick-start. We don't need them today because we have the Bible. It's really a silly way of practicing Christianity to me—a religion based on a miracle—but I'm guessing they don't have a cabinet full of self-addressed stamped envelopes.

Anyway, my brother-in-law says to my wife, "God woke me up. Now, initially, I thought it was just a bad slice of pizza." This is more like my brother-in-law. The voice of the Lord can be mistaken for indigestion. It's something to look out for. "But," he continues, "He woke me up again. I just felt like I was supposed to pray for you. So I did. I didn't really know what I was praying about, but I prayed for you."

Piecing together the timeline of events through a complicated process known as guessing, I discovered that he was praying around the same time that I was reminded of "seeing greater things."

This greater thing is named Eden Olivia. She's five years old at the time of this writing. Six in a month. (Seven by the time this book is finished. Twenty-eight by the time I receive a royalty check.)

We have learned so much from this experience. We have learned that doubt isn't a virtuous thing to be encouraged, nor is it a plague that will destroy our faith. It's just there. It's human—though distinctions must be made, hopefully with more analogies. When we sport doubt like a badge of honor, the pin that holds on the badge is unbelief.

Possibly skepticism.

We will never know.

It just goes to show you how patient God is with us. If He's patient with you, I can't say for sure; but He seems to be patient with us.

After finishing professional doubter Patton Dodd's book *My Faith So Far*, I wrote on the inside flap, "I get a little tired of hearing how certain Christians are more authentic than Christians who actually believe classic doctrinal statements. Believing seems to be off-putting to many Christians these days. Look, I'm no mountain-mover, but this doubting/authentic/ intellectually superior attitude is getting a little annoying to those of us who want to apply the Bible to our lives. Yes, I'm irritated by certain things in evangelicalism myself, but I'd still like to pray until I'm answered. Doubt takes away my prayer life. Can you leave me something?"[8]

We don't believe that unbelief is a sin anymore, which is ironic. We don't believe in unbelief. Really, it's the only sin for which people are condemned. If you're saved by faith alone, in the tradition of the Reformation, then you're damned by unbelief alone. (It has nothing to do with the fact that you laughed out loud during what was supposed to be a serious moment in one of the *Left Behind* movies.) Unbelief is the originator of all other sins. It is the most devastating of all grievances against God precisely because He is completely trustworthy.

Doubt becomes unbelief when we refuse to believe God in spite of experiencing numerous moments of His presence and goodness in our lives. Indeed, the downward spiral continues until you have to reinvent your faith to accommodate your unbelief or abandon it altogether along with your collection of Thomas Kincaid paintings.

C. H. Spurgeon put it this way: "Faith encourages every virtue; unbelief murders every one. Thousands of prayers have been strangled in their infancy by unbelief. Unbelief has been guilty of infanticide; it has murdered many an infant prayer; many songs of praise that would have swelled the chorus of the

---

8. *My Faith So Far* by Patton Dodd, scribbled on inside flap of the back cover by Thor Ramsey. Basically, I just quoted myself after writing in Patton Dodd's book. So, I'm not sure how helpful this footnote will be since I have the only copy with this reference.

skies have been stifled by an unbelieving murmur; many a noble enterprise conceived in the heart has been destroyed before it could come forth, by unbelief. Many men would have been missionaries; would have stood and preached their Master's gospel boldly; but they were filled with unbelief. Once a giant stops believing, he then becomes a dwarf."[9]

Whenever your faith is holding on by a thread that's about to snap, remember who will catch you when you fall from that cliff . . . the arms of God Himself. (I think I read that on a pillow with a doily border somewhere. People give you all kinds of stuff when you have a baby.)

Whatever doubts I have about my faith, they are within the context of the Resurrection of Christ, the one thing that I believe with a high degree of certitude. Christ lived, He died, He rose again. This makes everything possible.

Just because there's a doctor involved doesn't mean nothing miraculous occurs.

Dr. Werlin got paid.

That's a miracle.

God is involved in everything.

Don't doubt it for one second.

9. C. H. Spurgeon, "The Sin of Unbelief."

CHAPTER 5

God Is Not Your Spouse

(What God Is Like . . . Kind Of)

As a child, I idolized my dad, and it had nothing to do with the fact that he was a lot like Buddha in the sense that he also had quite a belly. Once, I actually asked my poor dad, "Dad, how come you're not a pro football player?" (Like it's a career choice for everyone. *Hmmm, should I be an overweight trucker or a multi-million-dollar quarterback?*)

What did I expect him to say? "Well, because I'm physically inferior to those other men. Son, it's time we had a little talk about genetics."

I always envied those kids who never had to lie about their parents' occupations. What a cruel thing for teachers to do—have you write a paper on what your parents do for a living and then read it in front of the entire class. "My dad hauls cattle and my mom empties bedpans for the elderly. Any questions?"

The reason I thought my dad could be a pro football player, though, is because I believed that my dad could do anything he wanted. I always admired my dad, and it had nothing to do with his cattle prod. Granted, I didn't know it as a kid, but my image of my father laid a foundation for my view of God, a foundation that is yet to pass municipal building codes.

I was discussing prison ministry with a pastor who told me about a local prison his church members visited regularly. (It's always a good idea for pastors to let their congregations know where the local prison is; that way, if there's ever a scandal, they know where to find him.) When Mother's Day rolled around, a local greeting card manufacturer offered the church's ministry all the card overages to give to the prisoners. "We couldn't keep up with the demand," the pastor said to me. "Everyone wanted a card to send to his mother."

This is amazing to me, because I think Mother's Day cards are among the hardest cards to buy, because they're all so fake. They all say something like: "To the most wonderful mother in the world." Why couldn't they just make a card that said, "You did the best you could"?

When Father's Day rolled around, this pastor thought they'd do the same thing for the prisoners. So, they made arrangements for the card manufacturer to deliver a large supply of Father's Day cards. "We couldn't give them away," the pastor told me. Then he said something that stuck with me: "I've never met a man in prison who doesn't hate his father."

This makes me want to cry, but I'm a man, so that's not going to happen.

One of the problems we have in our culture is that we look at our fathers and suspect that this is what God must be like, when we should actually think exactly the opposite. We should look at God as our Father and then yell at our dads. But the God as Father analogy eventually breaks down; so does the marriage analogy of understanding God, and every other analogy of understanding God for that matter. They all fail at some point, because *we're talking about God*, who said, "You thought I was altogether like you" (Ps. 50:21).

On the question of knowing God, there is a trend in the Emergent Church to look at God as a mysterious fuzz bomb, and if you find an actual reference in current theological literature that uses the phrase "fuzz bomb," you must contact me immediately because that will certainly embolden my thesis.

In this instance, however, they are correct. God *is* beyond us, and certainly incomprehensible to our minds. However (and please let me know if back-to-back howevers are too much), there comes a point when we treat God as so ultimately mysterious that it undermines our faith. You don't bow down and obey a vague mystery, unless she says, "Pick me up at seven." We cannot comprehend all that God is in Himself, but we can get a glimpse of what God is like. At least, the writers of the Bible seem to think so. We can't know much, but we can know something.

Various analogies are used to help us understand how God relates to us, and though they are well-intentioned, they often diminish God the same way a comedian often interrupts the flow of theological thought with a joke. All that any analogy can really do is give us a glimpse of God. A. W. Tozer wrote, in his gem of a little book *The Knowledge of the Holy*, "God is not like anything; that is, He is not *exactly* like anything or anybody."[1]

Well, except Jesus. God is just like Jesus.

For years now, I've started all my private prayers with, "Dear God, I pray to You as You are and not as I perceive You to be. Please replace my misconceptions about You with a clearer image of who You are." And then I ask for a Cadillac.

We need to know what God is like, because the greatest danger is coming to believe that God is different than He actually is.[2] This is why all these thoughts matter. And these are mighty important thoughts, so don't let my floppy shoes distract you.

Let's take a look at some of these analogies and see where they fall short and where they help us know what God is like.

---

1. A. W. Tozer, *The Knowledge of the Holy* (New York: HarperCollins Publishers, 1961), n.p.
2. Ibid.

God as Spouse

Our relationship with God is often compared to a marriage relationship; but God is not your spouse. We just have to keep reminding ourselves, "Theology is better than sex." My relationship with God is nothing like my relationship with my wife, except that most of the time I don't know what she's thinking either.

When people say that our relationship with God is like any other relationship, they have probably had better relationships than I have. Here's a good rule of thumb: The fewer relationships you have, the fewer people there are in the world who hate you. In reality, our relationship with God is *unlike* any other relationship, because who can compare to God? Who actually loves you unconditionally? Okay, besides your dog. Let me rephrase that question: Who actually has an I.Q. over 25 and loves you unconditionally? Who can be your closest friend and husband and brother? I know they try in Kentucky, but God is the only one who can be all things to us. My wife cannot be all things to me . . . but that doesn't mean she shouldn't try.

The other place the spousal model of God breaks down is in communication. When I need to speak to my wife, I sit her down and look her in the face. According to the Bible, if I did this with God, I would die. Sometimes my wife will give me one of those if-looks-could-kill looks, but it doesn't work for the very simple reason that she is not God.

Another area where our relationship with God is unlike any other relationship is in our craving for intimacy, to be known and understood by someone other than the local bartender. Because of our family history, my wife and I were both desperate to start a family. After only a week of dating, my wife told me that she loved me. And of course, I said, "Thank you." Now,

as much as I love my wife (though it was several weeks later)
I can't explain my inner self to her no matter how hard I try.
This is the paradox in our relationship with our Creator. I know
that I'm completely understood, but I do not come close to
understanding God. It's the silence that nags at us sometimes,
whereas in our human relationships it's just the opposite. It's
the nagging we'd like to silence.

There is less silence in human relationships. They provide
more immediate feedback compared to our relationship with
God. After I tell my wife what I'm thinking, she speaks and,
most often, speaks very clearly, though sometimes she rolls her
eyes. After I pray, there is often silence. Most Christians don't
hear God the way they hear their spouse or their next-door
neighbor; and when they claim they do, I suspect they go to a
Charismatic church. If my wife could read my every thought
and intention, there probably would be more silence in our
relationship and a lot more slaps across the face while at the
mall. God knows me completely, before there is a word on my
tongue or a woman in a skimpy halter top around the corner
from *Build-A-Bear*.[3]

God as Three Persons

Though God is a Person, He's beyond what personhood is to
you and me. God the Father, God the Son and God the Holy
Spirit are one Being, three Persons. I am a son, a father and a
husband; one person, three idiots. Okay, most analogies regarding the Triune nature of God do not work. The point is that God
is not a person in the same sense that we are, and it behooves

---

3. Note to Christian women in California: Wear clothes to church. When preachers
comment on how the women dress (or don't) in church, even the moms defend
their teenage daughters' hooker-wear with lines like, "This is California. We do
things differently here." Really? Well, men lust the same everywhere they go.

us to remember this, otherwise we end up with a smaller god, a god like one of us. And thank God that God is not like one of us; otherwise we would have to entertain the possibility of God being a slob or a jerk. Scary and not comforting. If God left His dirty clothes laying around, we could all suffocate. Not a god to be trusted. Small 'g' god.

Words fail us when speaking of the Trinity, but this doesn't mean the movie *The Matrix* was that much help either. Tozer says that the Trinity is a truth for the heart. Still, this shouldn't keep us from trying to explain the loftiness of the Godhead. When our words fall short, it often reveals just how great God is, because our hearts can take over where our words end. Beware, because when our hearts take over, this is when things like Barry Manilow's "Mandy" are created. So, as you can see, we should always keep our hearts and our minds attached whenever possible.

Our God is a majestic God, not easily understood, but often shoddily explained by the saying, "God is a big God." Our Green Giant theology sometimes annoys me. "We serve a big God," like He's some sort of large green man standing in a field of peas. How about revising this popular phrase to "We serve a God beyond big"? The words fail us. It's the best that we can do, I guess. We serve a big God, but we have small minds.

When God is loftier, then God's love is loftier too, and everything else that goes along with God's love, like the compassion and justice and holiness of God. That's why God is holy; He is other than we are, separate from us, unique to the point of evoking worship and inspiring three-chord praise songs.

The Trinity is one of the doctrines that elevates the Christian concept of God above your average deity, because it makes God Himself a family.

God as Family

You ever show up at a family reunion and ask, "Who's that guy?"

"That's your mother's new husband."

"Oh, it's always a pleasure to meet one of my mother's new husbands."

Both my wife and I come from extremely fractured families. I have three half-brothers and two half-sisters, but they don't refer to me as their half-brother because it's such an odd-sounding phrase. Instead, they call me "freak of nature."

One of my brothers is only seven years younger than my mother. It's not her kid. He is what we call my dad's Senior Prom baby.

We were a family-type group.

Hey, I'm all for variations, but what's wrong with a standard? I think this whole nuclear family thing is a good idea. You've got a dad, a mom and a sister. What's wrong with that? It just makes it easier to introduce them to people. If your family is anything like mine, it gets confusing. "Ah, yeah, this is my dad, my stepdad, my dad's 'friend,' my mom, my stepmother, my half-brother from my dad's third wife, my Fairy godmother, my evil stepsister, Uncle Joe and Auntie Frank, and the foster elf who's riding a donkey. That's my family. Quick—take a picture."

That's why no one sends Christmas cards anymore. It's too complicated.

The Godhead gives us a loving model of a trusting family where no one fights about doing the dishes. The idea that God is love didn't even come into play until the apostle John wrote it in a New Testament letter called First John, a letter he wrote with the assumption that he would write a sequel. God is love—this is a New Testament revelation. Once Christ had come to Earth, He could more fully reveal God. This is where Christianity departs from Islam and Judaism. Their God is not in eternal relationship. He's not family. It's not just that God is your spouse; He's your entire family. God is always more, never less. If Christ is our Brother, He is also our King, our Counselor, our Supplier, our Judge, our Scapegoat, our Greatest Fan, and so forth.

God is always more.

If God is family, then when people walk into your church or home or attend your small group, they should be made to feel like family, whether they are born again or not. They should be made to feel loved whether they are Buddhist or gay or black or Jewish or conservative judgmental Christians (I want love, too). If loving people doesn't come easy to you, then find some other people.

Pretend you're in a church service and the pastor is about to read some funny Internet sayings. Here are some things you can say to people to make them feel loved and welcome, whether they are or not:

- Hold a mirror up to their nose and say, "It looks like you're still breathing. How bad can it be?"

- "We're all very accepting here . . . but then again we all know each other. Good luck fitting in."

- Put your arm on their shoulder and say, "I just want you to know that if you ever need someone, I'm here for you . . . until the service is over, then you're on your own."

- "I hope you feel welcome here, because . . . you'd be the first and that would be kind of encouraging to *us*."

- "Nobody here is perfect, but there is no excuse for that outfit. What were you thinking?"

- "You have a really kind face. Can you give me some money?"

- "I love everybody. And soon you'll find that very annoying."

The very heart of the Trinity is others-oriented relationship. This is why Christ came to give His life as a ransom for many. It was an idea foreign to Greek culture at that time. Dennis Kinlaw writes, in his book from which I have lifted most of these ideas, "For Jesus' love is the giving of oneself to and for the one loved. Greek has no word to express that thought because such a thought is not natural to human beings as we know human beings."[4]

Still, "Honey, such a thought is not natural to human beings" is no answer to give your spouse when she asks, "Do you love me?"

God as Male

Because sex so defines who we are as people, it seems unnatural for us to think of an existence without it; but God is not a sexual Being. God created sex, and this is why the phrase "God is good" originated. Though God Himself has no sexuality.

Thus, God is not a man but could certainly kick your butt if needed. I wonder how Jesus responded to the kid who bragged, "I bet my dad could beat up your dad."

"My Dad created your dad."

God is not a woman but is certainly regarded as a Designer and is very much like a woman in the sense that He has rules about adultery, too.

---

4. Dennis F. Kinlaw, *Let's Start with Jesus: A New Way of Doing Theology* (Grand Rapids, MI: Zondervan, 2005), p. 30.

The personal pronoun "he" is used to describe God because men dominated society at the time the *King James Bible* was translated. The personal pronoun "he" is also used to describe God because God likes men better than women. I have no theological basis for this. It's just a hunch. My wife said that God doesn't play favorites, and I nodded in agreement as I looked toward the sky and winked. Then a bird pooped on my head.

Most theologians would agree that God is described in the Bible in human terms to help us understand God, and to understand God's ways with God's people. They would also agree that the continual use of the word "God" to describe God and God's ways with God's people without the use of a personal pronoun is annoying.

Some of the character descriptions of God in the Bible are male, such as the previously discussed God as Father; and others are female, such as a hen gathering up her chicks (see Matt. 23:37; Isa. 66:13). Still, most theologians would have a cow if you called God "her" from the pulpit, let alone "Mother Hen." This could lead to a rambunctious chat about women in ministry, an issue that is not essential to the gospel, even though many theologians treat it so. It's not something I will cover here because there are many pastors who are open to having a comedian in their church, and I want them to hire me.

Suffice it to say that Catherine Booth, the cofounder of the Salvation Army, wrote a chapter in one of her books in defense of women preaching the gospel, and it destroyed her career as a comedian. However, if there are theological debates in the kingdom of heaven when she takes on "male preachers only" theologian Wayne Grudem, I'll be putting some bets down—if betting is allowed in heaven, assuming that money will be needed for some reason. (If there are streets of gold, I hope the dollar still has value. Otherwise, what's the point really?)

Actually, trying to attribute a sexual identity to God only shows how little we think of God and how much our metaphors fail us. I imagine that some of the hubbub over God's gender stems from the fact that Jesus was God in the flesh. This doesn't mean that God is male. It just means that God understands the cultural context of history. If you think women are underpaid now, just go back 2,000 years. Or move to Iraq. God showed up as a man, and we killed Him. What would we have done to a woman?

God as Messiah

In the Old Testament, Israel calls God "Father" (see Deut. 32:6; Isa. 63:16; 64:8). They were most often a stubborn and rebellious people, so I'm sure they called Him other things too, but the prophets who liked God thought it best to omit those remarks. And the nation of Israel is called God's "firstborn." So, God wants to have more children. (If you just keep trying, hopefully one will turn out decent. We stopped at one. You can't beat perfection.) Interestingly, Israel is God's firstborn, even though Christ speaks of God as His Father. But then, as part of the Godhead, Christ has always been in relationship with His Father. He was begotten as Mary's baby, and He grew up as a man to bring us a fuller revelation of God's character, and some well-made furniture. If we look at Jesus, we see a brighter image of God. It's not that the Old Testament God is a different God than the New Testament God. It's just that the New Testament image is more vivid. Jesus is God's Highlighter. It's the difference between watching home movies and actually touching the people filmed.

Recently, I was watching home movies from my childhood that I had transferred onto DVD, which should have been some sort of document of our lives; but 20 years later, you only get to see yourself at age 8 for a millisecond, because your dad's going, "Get outta the way. I'm trying to film that tree." My dad filmed scenery. My mom cut off our heads. I don't know what I looked like as a kid, but I can tell you that in the third grade I had suede Buster Brown shoes. If you watch our old home movies you wouldn't even know these people had children. My dad actually filmed the road while driving once. I guess that way if he got lost, he wouldn't have to ask directions—he could just review the film.

You can tell family vacations were stressful events without even seeing the actual people. My dad filming the road. A big green sign, "Orlando 78 miles." He pans over to a big white sign with red letters, "Discount Liquor." The camera crashes into the dash as he slams on the brakes.

They did film me as a baby, however. They got all the big events. There I am after my bath, lying naked on the carpet, sucking on a bottle. There I am after graduation, lying naked on the carpet, sucking on a bottle.

While you're watching old home movies, do you ever say to yourself, "I don't remember any of these people?" It's when my brother was gunned down at a tollbooth that I realized . . . I put in *The Godfather* by mistake. Ba-da-bing. The point is, home movies give us an incomplete picture of our family. They're just glimpses of some of the big moments, along with some of the small. People need to meet our families in the flesh to really be appalled by them.

In the same respect, if you only look at the Old Testament revelation of God, it's incomplete without Christ, who is an eternal member of the Godhead. God is more hidden in the Old Testament—active, but not as fully revealed to the nations. God is one, but God is family: Father, Son and Holy Spirit. God is eternal, co-existing, self-giving and intimate. And once your spouse finds this out, it really puts the pressure on your marriage.

Baggage accompanies all our best efforts in communicating truth about God. Even God fully expressing Himself in Christ came with the baggage of our humanity.

This fact alone explains love handles.

God as Mysterious

Sometimes we know, but we don't know how we know. We know that we know only because of God's Spirit, but we don't know why we know. God is mysterious, but we have to know something about Him in order to interact with Him. Thus, God has revealed Himself to humanity in the Person of Jesus Christ, but because of the vast gulf between the infinite God and people who actually enjoyed the movie remake of *The Dukes of Hazard*, the clear vision with which our hearts sometimes see God remains a mystery, as do many box-office hits. The mystery will always humble us. It remains a mystery why Jesus wrote in the dust while He spoke to a group that was about to stone a woman caught in adultery. We know for certain that He did not condemn this woman nor condone her adultery, something few of us can do simultaneously. There is mystery and there is certainty. We know when we have met God. We know when God is present and when His Spirit is absent.

We know that God is love.

God as Love

One of the most compelling descriptions of God's care for us is found in the Gospel of Matthew, where the author writes, "If you then, though you are evil, know how to give good gifts to your children, how much more will your Father in heaven give good gifts to those who ask him!" (7:11). I'm not sure what kind of gifts parents gave their children 2,000 years ago. This is probably where the pet-rock craze started, but one thing is sure, parents have always wanted to bless their children with gifts.

I have a six-year-old daughter named Eden. (That's how long this book has taken. She just turned seven.) She is named after the Garden before the Fall because she's perfect. I never make jokes about my daughter, unless they're jokes about her being perfect to me, because I never want her to know anything but my complete and utter love for her. I never want her to doubt the depths of my love. For her, I would give my life. Despite whatever difficulties we encounter in our marriage, my wife and I continue to love each other, and this is a gift to our child. In a similar way, this is why God loves the Son and the Son loves the Father to the point of obedience unto death—as a gift to their children, to you and me.

No joke.

CHAPTER 6

The Beginning of Narcissism

(Theology of Why Mean People Suck)

Freud believed that guilt was the result of a caveman murdering his father. And, of course, the most common objection theologians give to this explanation is, "Well, *you* didn't know his father. You'd have killed him too." Still, Freud's explanation for guilt doesn't explain why the caveman felt guilty in the first place.[1] A better explanation for the caveman's guilt might be that the caveman had a mother whom he never called, which is where many believe that guilt originated.

From a Christian standpoint, guilt is just evidence that we have stubbed our soul by walking where we shouldn't have. In other words, we have sinned.

Calling someone out for his or her sins is tricky business, especially if you don't know how to operate a bullhorn. There was a time when Christians called out sinners, not only by name, but also by their particular sins. The apostle Paul wrote in 1 Corinthians, "Expel the wicked man from among you" (1 Cor. 5:13). Our church doesn't even have detention, let alone expulsion. Now, I'm not advocating a return to this practice carte blanche,

---

1. Peter Kreeft, "The Pillars of Unbelief—Freud," *The National Catholic Register*, January-February 1988. http://www.catholiceducation.org/articles/civilization/cc0012.html (accessed December 2007).

but only when it comes to my mother's ex-husband, Steve McReynolds, and my former fiancée, Sandy Berhman, who is actually a fictional character, but still, cheating is wrong regardless of the context.

Objections will arise, I am certain, from some who feel strongly that I shouldn't use my former stepfather's real name, so I have changed his actual last name, which is McAllen, to the fictitious name McReynolds. This way, he remains anonymous and I can still rebuke him for his narcissism via comedy.

There is a reason the therapist has replaced the pastor in our society. The therapist probably won't call my problems sin, and she certainly better not call me a narcissist, that is, unless she's very insightful. I've always been suspicious of therapy myself, but my suspicion is probably just a chemical imbalance. Now, I'm not against therapy, as long as someone else is paying for it. Doubtless, it has become quite obvious to me (which is why it's doubtless) that the language of therapy has replaced the language of theology in parts of the Church. It's an old argument made by sweaty preachers who yell too much, but this makes it no less true, even when you sit in the front row and the speaker accidentally spits on you. Still, the language of therapy drives our society. Phrases like, "I'm trying to salvage my marriage." *You're trying to salvage your marriage? Sounds to me like you're going to a relationship dump to look for parts.*

"Yeah, I'm looking for some understanding on an '83 unendorsed elope."

"No, all I've got on hand is a '76 marriage with a couple of affairs and some nagging left."

Not that the language of therapy contains no theological truth. I think narcissism is a very good description of what ails the vast majority of human beings, even outside of Hollywood.

When Adam and Eve turned from God, this was the beginning of narcissism. They went from being God-centered to being self-centered. This self-centeredness is responsible for most of the ills in our world—from wars to poverty to boy bands.

Personally, I think that a world in which humanity has turned away from God and become spiritually blind and morally corrupt is a much better explanation for our current state of affairs than neurotransmitters. Not that neurotransmitters shouldn't be carefully studied. They just don't make you feel the good kind of guilt. Now, what I mean by the good kind of guilt is simply actions and thoughts that we *should* feel guilty about because they are unkind or cruel or proud, etc. It's the basic theory of Christianity: People suck because they're sinners. This is why repentance is a better prescriptive than St. John's Wort.

There was a time, before I became a Christian, when I thought therapy and psychiatrists were fine and dandy; but once you question the premise of your world view and find it wanting, as I did when contemplating this whole conversion process, suddenly you're not afraid to point out all the naked emperors running around. If you envy the naked emperors—now you're in Freud's territory.

One thing I do love about Freud, though, is his complete honesty. Harvard professor Dr. Armand M. Nicholi, Jr., in his amazingly insightful and readable book, *The Question of God*, which parallels and debates the views of Freud with those of Christian apologist and author C. S. Lewis, observed that Freud said, "Psychoanalysis has not made the analysts themselves better, nobler, or of stronger character."[2] So, therapy doesn't even help the therapists.

This isn't to say I dismiss therapy outright. That's not the case at all. I dismiss it more backhandedly. Mental health is no

---

2. Dr. Armand M. Nicholi, Jr., *The Question of God: C. S. Lewis and Sigmund Freud Debate God, Love, Sex and the Meaning of Life* (New York: Simon and Schuster, 2002), p. 64.

laughing matter, because when people are depressed, they don't laugh. As a comedian, I think we should do everything we can to fight this dreaded disease. If you got pills, take 'em—unless you're suicidal; then I need to clarify that I mean *take them one at a time*, not by the handful.

It was on a therapist's couch that I began contemplating the nature of sin, because sin isn't as sinful when you're sitting on a nice leather couch.

Before my wife and I underwent in vitro fertilization, we were required to undergo mandatory couples' therapy. Apparently, if you can have children naturally, you can be nuts. But if you need the assistance of science, they want to make sure all your marbles are in a row, or wherever it is the shrinks want your marbles to be.

So, we go to therapy.

By force.

We sit there in a pretend living room, wanting this complete stranger to like us, so of course we're not ourselves. We form this corporate personality to impress this lady. Personalities that have nothing to do with our real personalities, because if she knew our real personalities, well, she might think we're nuts; and who wants their therapist thinking they're nuts?

She was a very pleasant lady, this therapist—late forties, plump, Cover-girl skin, but thinning Superman-colored hair, a dark, shiny, comic-book blue. According to some of the photos in her office, in college she had this full, wavy foliage that is now only shy curls not wanting to make a fuss over covering her scalp. (Sorry. I was reading some Donald Miller earlier.)

She asked about our family history, how our parents communicated, probing to see what kind of role models we had. As I told about my family—Grandpa the Nazi, Dad the Dog Killer—I could tell by her face that she felt she had some new long-term customers.

"Are you ever depressed?" asked the nice therapist with Super-hair.

I'm probably manic-depressive and that's the reason I don't see a psychiatrist. I don't want it to be official. Still, it doesn't interfere with my life. And being manic-depressive in the arts probably helps.

So, that's my answer.

"Yeah, and it helps."

"Does anyone in your family see a therapist?"

Several people I know see a therapist regularly, have for years, but I adamantly deny that there is a correlation between knowing me and seeing a therapist.

"Look, we're just here because we want to have a baby," is what I want to say, but don't. Instead we give her a list of 20 or so relatives. She calls them "leads."

She asks my wife, "Do you ever feel you have narcissistic tendencies?" This really insults me, because I'm sitting there thinking, *What about* my *tendencies?*

Super-hair then asks us a series of questions about each other. I don't actually recall what my wife's answer was in response to, but she said, "Oh, he's an insomniac." This really makes me angry, internally. On the outside, I'm dazzling a smile to blind even the angels unaware. On the inside, fire and brimstone.

I'm not an insomniac. I'm a late person. I go to bed late; around 1:00 or 2:00 in the morning, and this is why I'm often greeted in the morning with remarks like, "I'm glad you decided to get up."

Decided to get up?

I don't decide to get up. I pretty much just sleep until I'm done. After you wake up, if you can go back to sleep, then you're not done. I'm not an insomniac. Honestly, I love to sleep. I love it. I have dreams about taking naps.

This is how most of the session goes. My wife tells the therapist something that I feel is grossly inaccurate, and I just sit there steaming about it with a nuclear smile. After the session is over, we go to the car and fight about all the things we couldn't say to each other in front of the therapist. I wondered to myself if the therapist somehow orchestrated this situation so that we'd have to come back. If you leave in worse shape than before you came, you have to go back. This is the therapy racket.

Afterwards, I said to my wife, "I hated myself before I saw a therapist; now I just hate myself with more clarity."

It's a never-ending cycle really. You go back, and more internal phlegm comes to the surface. It's often discouraging, especially if all that's deep inside is phlegm. Can the therapist reach inside and change my phlegm into something wonderful?

Please don't misunderstand my cynicism. I believe Superhair, Ph.D., clinical psychologist, helped us understand our phlegm. I just think she was powerless to change it.

Theology is just as practical.

Now, I'm not saying there is no benefit to therapy; for the most part, therapy has become our national religion. All I'm proposing is that you give theology a chance at your disorder. In my opinion, you have a better chance with God than with Freud.

Freud is dead.

God is dead—but only for three days. (Will you buy that if I put it on a T-shirt?)

At least God worked better for me when I was suffering from what has become a common neurosis. I used to suffer from obsessive-compulsive disorder, currently known as the hand-washing disease where people compulsively wash their hands over and over again.

I didn't suffer from compulsive hand washing.

Still don't.

"Pleasure to meet you. Shake?"

I didn't know it was obsessive-compulsive behavior as a kid, though several of my third-grade peers did diagnose me as weird.

It all started with a helpful youngster who hipped me to the fact that "if you step on a crack you break your mother's back." I had no idea I was the one responsible for her lumbago.

So, I began walking over all cracks with a compulsion, you might say.

I lived in a small town, and many of the sidewalks were buckled from the root systems of trees with secrets, the leaves whispering with the bygone gossip of couples they shaded.[3] These sections of sidewalk had hundreds of cracks. I couldn't just jump over one section onto the next slab. No, this was cheating somehow. I had to hit the space between each small crack in the slab. So, walking home from school, suddenly I'd launch into my best Baryshnikov routine and tiptoe over each crack.

I was asked on several occasions, "What are you doing?"

What was I to say?

"Oh, I'm probably nuts. I just don't know what to call it yet."

I told the inquirers it was just a game I played.

"Well, how do you play it?"

"You have to step over each crack without touching it."

"Why?"

"So your mother won't have to endure physical therapy."

This soon advanced (as compulsions always do when you indulge them) into a more complex compulsion that involved imaginary lines that ran from telephone poles and crossed the street. I'd sit in the back seat of the car and lift my feet with perfect timing to avoid the invisible telephone pole lines. This soon became a burden, because according to the number of poles we passed, telephones are widely used.

So I had to develop a different strategy.

---

3. Sorry about that. I was reading a little *Through Painted Deserts* this morning, thus the "Donald Miller Moment." Again.

My new strategy involved allowing several poles to pass without lifting my feet. The lines would grab my ankles and follow with the car as my feet stretched them like the string of a bow and arrow. As we passed more and more poles, the tension from the lines became stronger and stronger until I lifted my feet, snapping them back into place. Using this strategy, I could ride in the car without having to lift my feet as often, only having to endure imaginary line tension.

As I matured, my compulsion presented me with new difficulties.

During high school football, this compulsion to avoid lines presented quite a problem, since football is played on a gridiron, a series of lines drawn on the field.

I was doomed.

After running a play, you can't just lift your feet and have the imaginary lines snap back into place because, well, for one thing, you have cleats on. For another thing, you're nuts. You're following the rules of some obsessive-compulsive universe that only exists in your head. But even us crazy people still operate within our worlds based on some type of reason. *There must be another way to rid my feet of these excess lines,* I thought to myself.

I don't remember how I developed the cure for chalk lines from holding my feet back, but what's important is that I developed a method of temporary relief from imaginary line tension on football fields even though I have yet to receive any credit for this medical breakthrough. However, I can't be petty if my cure will help others, so I will share it with you now (unaccredited by the scientific community).

Before I took my stance for the next play, I swiped the bottom tip of my shoes with each hand and then blew the imaginary lines away with a puff of breath. Yes, ladies and gentlemen, it's as simple as that to relieve your feet of imaginary line tension. Just swipe and blow. The only thing you need to be careful of while using this technique is illegal motion in the backfield. On several occasions, I was called for illegal motion because sometimes I couldn't get it just right on the first swipe and blow. I had to do several swipe and blows until it felt right.

This compulsion followed me into college where I eventually believed in the teachings of Jesus. And this probably explains why I am Protestant. Catholicism would have been my undoing. Kneel, dip, sign of the cross, kneel, dip, sign of the cross, kneel, stick out tongue, chew, etc.

Well, what's an obsessive-compulsive Protestant to do?

While reading the Bible, I came to believe that my obsessive habits were a type of superstition.[4] I was trusting in these rituals. If I didn't perform them, who knows what might happen? How can you run for a touchdown when you have miles and miles of imaginary lines holding your feet back? I had to swipe and blow. I couldn't risk the consequences, for the sake of the team. The swiping and blowing was a bizarre way of achieving a very temporary peace of mind, a peace of mind that often only lasted for seconds. This to me was superstition, which I believe God frowns on. I reasoned, *If I am trusting in these superstitious compulsions to help me through the day, then I am not trusting in Christ to help me through the day.*

Even though I felt that the world would soon spin backward out of control if I didn't free my shoes of the imaginary line tension, I felt more strongly that I should trust in Jesus Christ to make my path straight instead of trusting in my own compulsions. Whenever I had the urge to step over cracks or swipe and blow, I just reminded myself that Someone else was in charge of my life.

---

4. I'm sure that some of you reading this (who do not share my faith) may find this statement funny. "He's exchanging one superstition for another." Religion itself is seen as superstition to some, so I feel it is only appropriate to tap my left shoulder three times with my right hand so that their views will not influence me.

As I resisted them, the compulsions grew weaker.

Soon I was free of this habit.

That, my friend, is theology as a cure for obsessive-compulsive disorder. It's why theology is more than just "ignorance with wings." It deals with the sovereignty of God in determining the direction of our lives. It deals with the choices we make to exercise faith in the goodness of God's sovereignty. It deals with one of many clinical names for idolatry.

The reason that therapy can aid theology is because some of the underlying premises are the same.

For example, the basic Christian theological story is that in the beginning, things were peachy. All-you-can-eat peaches; just stay away from the apple tree. It wasn't actually an apple tree. It was the Tree of the Knowledge of Good and Evil, which are never in season. Eat everything else in the garden, God tells them. *Everything* else. They only had to deny themselves one tree. Idiots. They ate of the tree. J. I. Packer wrote, in his Reformed-leaning but still useful little volume *Concise Theology*, "By eating from this tree Adam would, in effect, be claiming that he could know and decide what was good and evil for him without any reference to God." Then he and Eve passed this genetic preponderance down to their progeny. So, you see, our problems are biological and chemical after all.

I recant.

What this episode of theological history teaches us (as does therapy) is that, in all honesty, sometimes our parents *are* to blame. Ask any sitcom writer and they will tell you they are screwed up because of their parents. Parents have tremendous influence over the lives of their children, for good or ill. Therapists have it right—sometimes it is your mother's fault. As children, we are victims of their idiocy. Then we grow up and perpetuate the same idiocy on other people's lives.

Now we're guilty.

You see, it's a premise problem. Some believe that people are screwed up because of biological or chemical problems. People go to a therapist because they are screwed up, on this we agree. But people are screwed up because of their parents. And their parents are screwed up because of their parents.

Basically, it's Adam's fault.

My objection to therapy, once again, is the language. This is where therapy fails us, in the naming of our sins. Sin is the reason people are screwed up, and when you deny sin, you deny what will really be helpful to all of us screwed-up people.

People hate calling sin, sin, especially if her name is Candy.

Welcome to Vegas!

In Carson City, Nevada, a judge called a man's 800 images of child porn an issue of impulse control, which is a bit like grandma polishing off a bottle of Vodka and then saying, "I'm just a little nervous." *Yeah, I think you're stinkin' nervous, Grandma.*

That's the kind of language tweaking I'm talking about. Call it what it is—an uprising of the heart and soul against the God who is good.

Look, people suck because they're sinners.

But there is hope. God has come that we might suck less.

Whenever some Christians talk about sin, they say, "Sin is sin to God." And Christians should know, because they're awfully good at it. (Notice the strategic distancing of myself from Christians here.) They also say things like, "God doesn't see my sin; He sees Jesus in my place." No, if you're abusing women, or embezzling from work or secretly vomiting behind your friend's couch during a party, God sees it. God is not an ostrich, and the atonement isn't a blindfold.

Saying "sin is sin" is a bit like saying "ugly is ugly." Now, we all know someone ugly and we all know someone UGLY! Sin is sin, as if God doesn't make a distinction between child molesters and mean drunks. People don't picket the homes of mean drunks with signs reading, "Leave our neighborhood, Steve McReynolds," unless they happen to live with him. Most people who don't attend church will tell you that sin isn't sin. (It often pays to listen to those who haven't been indoctrinated, because their thinking is sometimes clearer.)

God sees sins as equal only in the sense that if you're willing to steal a small thing, then you're probably willing to steal a large thing—the only question being how you will fit it in your pants. It's the state of the heart, once again, that is God's concern. Initially, all sin is internal before it's external. For example, murder is just anger communicated really well. And this is why you should never have an affair with a large woman, because her husband is probably large, too. However, a small angry man with a gun can be just as lethal. So, affairs overall should be pooh-poohed and not just for moral reasons. They're bad for your health, as murder generally is.

The point that the "sin is sin" crowd is trying to make is that the core of all sin is selfishness; so just because your selfishness is on a smaller scale than a mean drunk's, don't think it's any less offensive to God. But enough about my mother's ex-husband.

People feel safer with a therapist because they pay them. Money makes people feel safer than "I won't tell." The mob calls it hush money. You can call it a bill, but either way, you feel safer.

Confession is good for the soul, but the cash keeps them quiet.

Personally, I think we Protestants made a grave mistake by getting rid of the confessional. It's good to have someone you can speak honestly to who is restricted from blabbing about it. Plus, the confessional has that little screen to make you feel like the priest can't see you. When Protestants confess their sins to someone, the pastor's big face is right there in front of you. How about a little mood lighting at least? Plus, where's the certainty that you won't be the subject of your pastor's next dinner conversation? Even the therapist can lose his/her license if he/she violates the patient/doctor privilege. What happens to the Protestant pastor? How effective is the reprimand, "Hey, you really shouldn't gossip!"

"Okay, I'll try and curb that."

The mystery is that to really feel loved by another human being, we have to reveal ourselves. The more fully you reveal your true self without hiding behind whatever it is you hide behind, the more fully you will feel loved by that person. It's God's model for intimacy. If you keep hiding, you will always struggle with the insecurity that he or she or they don't really love you. Well, they can't love you if they don't really know you, now can they?

This is why when we hide our sins, we feel alone.

God has never been impressed with our self-marketing, our glittery take on the truth, which is basically a flashy form of fibbing. (I have discovered that it's okay to fib in church as long as you call it marketing.)

But confession to a therapist or priest or pastor's big head is ultimately dissatisfying if not preceded with confession to Christ. The reason we feel the need to confess to a person is because innately we have the need to confess to God.

We need to be forgiven.

Freud had the guilt thing right.

CHAPTER 7

My God Is Bigger Than Your god

(and Now for Something Really Offensive)

I'm not sure of many things (because I don't want to commit the gravest sin in the emerging church, which is being certain of anything), but the one thing I am certain of is this: If we lose the exclusiveness of Christ, we lose the ability to really offend people. Sure you can offend people by telling them their mother wears army boots; well, I guess that's not really offensive anymore now that women serve in the military. My point is, if you really want to offend someone these days, tell them they cannot get to heaven, regardless of how much traction their army boots have, without Jesus Christ. If you have to, take them out to the parking lot and point to your bumper sticker: "No Jesus, no salvation. Know Jesus, know salva." (Obviously, someone tried to peel off your bumper sticker.)

I am concerned with some of the fuzzy thinking in the Church these days, because I hate it when my velvet jacket gets covered with lint, but that's what you get with fuzzy thinking. For example, one popular author and speaker said, "Jesus is the only Savior, but not everybody who is being saved by Him is aware that He is the one who is doing the saving."[1]

---

1. Tony Campolo, *EP News Service*, October 4, 1985.

Well, that certainly takes the pressure off evangelists.

"I'm a practicing Hindu."

"Fine, but you're being saved by Jesus."

"No. I don't think so."

"You just don't know it. Next."

"Wait. Why am I not aware of Christ saving me?"

"Well, I'm sure He doesn't want to offend you."

We live in a culture that has no concept of offending someone for the sake of love. Love is speaking softly, smiling brightly and not correcting anyone. That's your grandma. That's not love. After most kids spend too much time with Grandma, they come home acting like brats. Now, I don't know if this has anything to do with the fact that when Grandma cuts your hair, she ends up slapping you in the head with that pulpy nannerhide she has floating under her arms; but God's love is not permissive, nor is there excess body fat involved. Sure, God ends up smacking us upside the head with Truth once in a while, but it's always balanced with love and it's never random like Mema's dangle meat. If only we could balance kicking people in the butt with love. It's a worthy goal. So, in this chapter, you will definitely feel my love.

Personally, I like it when someone stirs me up, especially if it has to do with my faith. That's why I read all of the books by Brian McLaren, the very influential and controversial Emergent Church Caucasian. He makes me think, question, search things out and eventually throw things. So, in this chapter I have only one goal—to make you throw one of Brian McLaren's books.

You see, as humans, we tend to overcorrect. Say for instance, a woman has a bad experience with a man, and she becomes a lesbian. That is overcorrecting. Or if someone is raised by a mother whose house is spotless, but he or she becomes a slob. In the same vein, sometimes people overcorrect theologically, such as someone who is reared in a fundamentalist Christian home believing that Jesus is the only way to heaven but never witnesses others in the home showing compassion toward outsiders. When he overcorrects, suddenly he's a Christian Universalist. Now, he has to replace his Christian bumper sticker that says, "It's not about the bunny," with a sticker that says, "What's the freaking point?" Because that's the kind of hope that universalism brings.

In this chapter, I will be overcorrecting in the opposite direction concerning the supremacy of Christ, with the idea that you have to believe in your heart and confess with your mouth that Jesus Christ is Lord (see Rom. 10:19). In other words, you have to be conscious of the fact that Christ is saving you—no Christian vegetables in this theological point of view.

Since lots of people feel that religion is a matter of personal preference, like food or color of clothing, they view the sentiment that Christ is supreme compared to all other religious leaders as arrogant or ignorant, especially if you're wearing a Christian T-shirt that says, "Don't believe in hell? It's still there. You're still going." (We've got thousands of these. Aren't they effective?)

So, let me just state for the record that I like Buddha. You get to rub his belly. That's kind of cute. Kind of like a sacred doughboy. And Buddhists are really peaceful and cool, and I bet if they hit your parked car by accident, they would leave a note. But Buddha can't forgive your sins. (I know. It's a drawback.)

Many church leaders feel that the subject of Christ's exclusivity should be avoided altogether. Instead, let seekers stumble upon that little truth by themselves and hope things work out. Focus on finding some common ground with those outside the church, they urge. Now, I agree with the common-ground aspect. I love miniature golf, as do many Buddhists. But when you thoughtfully explain to people the good reasons for believing in the exclusivity of Christ, sometimes they still think you're an arrogant ignoramus. Then again, it might be your

T-shirt. Expressing this sentiment probably doesn't help when you're wearing a garment that says, "Christ died so you could suck less."

There is not only a sheepishness now in our proclamation of the gospel, but we're so afraid of the supremacy-of-Christ issue that many church leaders are not only leaning toward Christian universalism, but some are also fully embracing it. Spencer Burke and Barry Taylor basically believe that everyone is already saved unless they choose not to be saved. They write in their book *A Heretic's Guide to Eternity*, "We're in unless we choose to opt out. . . . We don't get grace because we're sinners."[2] But if we weren't sinners, we wouldn't need grace to begin with. It's really a silly theology, but it is consistent with the idea that you're being saved but you just don't know it. If you remain ignorant, I guess there's no chance of opting out. We should just shut up about this whole gospel thing before someone loses his salvation.

Spencer is a Universalist who believes in hell, which is kind of like being a stripper who believes in modesty. Spencer writes, "I certainly don't want to build a case for hell on the basis of one snippet of Scripture."[3] But he's willing to build a case for universalism on the basis of no snippets of Scripture and in spite of all the verses about hell. He then writes, "We live in an age where there truly is never one answer to any question, whether it's about God or cornflakes!"[4] This is intriguing to me because I truly would like to know the many answers to the issue of cornflakes. Is this a pressing concern for people? "I'm running late because I can't answer the question—plain or frosted?"

---

2. Spencer Burke and Barry Taylor, *A Heretic's Guide to Eternity* (San Francisco: Jossey-Bass, 2006), p. 202.

3. Ibid., p. 199.

4. Ibid., p. 142.

Now, don't get me wrong (again). Spencer is probably a nice guy who would be a great Starbucks conversationalist; as we chatted over green tea frappuccinos, I would lovingly needle him about his theology as the comments progressively became more pointed, until he cried like a little girl and repented of his theological idiocy. It's just what I do to people I love.

This outlook is becoming more common than a youth pastor with a goatee. The members of a self-proclaimed emerging Church of the Apostles in Seattle write, "We do not possess truth or seek to correct the truths of others, but we seek to live faithfully in light of the truth of God in Jesus Christ."[5] Now, there's a sentence to unpack. Here's what I understand they are saying. Okay, this church has no truth. (Maybe they should buy a Bible.) Others have what they believe to be the truth, but this church feels that's none of its business, which is odd because many of the New Testament letters were written to "correct the truths of others."[6] This church claims they'll just live by what they believe to be the truth of God in Jesus Christ, apparently oblivious to verses about salvation being found in no one else but Jesus Christ. But that's what you get from a church without Bibles.

Not that reciting Bible verses will be enough. It's completely true that information doesn't win people over; love does. So the next time you find yourself quoting John 14:6 to someone, where Jesus says, "I am the way, the truth and the life, no one comes to the Father except by me," make sure you hand them a teddy bear afterwards. The Bible tells us to speak the truth in love (see Eph. 4:15). I think this can only mean to hand out stuffed animals with unpleasant Scriptures.

5. Mark Driscoll, John Burke, Dan Kimball, Doug Pagitt and Karen Ward, *Listening to the Beliefs of Emerging Churches: Five Perspectives* (Grand Rapids, MI: Zondervan, 2007), p. 179.

6. I found John McArthur's book *The Truth War: Fighting for Certainty in an Age of Deception* very helpful in this respect (Nashville, TN: Thomas Nelson, 2007).

Why are we so afraid to stand up and shout, "Jesus Christ is superior to all other religious leaders, and that means you, Muhammad," in a local mosque? Okay, just because you have convictions doesn't mean you should do something stupid. You would be an idiot for shouting this in a mosque. Have it printed on a placard and stand across the street, of course.

Now, just because I believe that Jesus Christ is the only way to heaven doesn't mean I can't enjoy a nice round of miniature golf with a Buddhist. And it doesn't mean I can't learn anything from a Buddhist either. 72 to 105. He kicked my butt. Because my Buddhist friend and I practice tolerance, we can discuss our differences openly without fisticuffs. (But if I'm going to duke it out with someone from another faith, I'll take my chances against a Buddhist. Those robes limit their mobility.)

One of my good friends is a Palestinian Christian. Honestly, I don't know how he gets through Psalms. He must take a Sharpie and blacken out the words "Israel" and "Zion" all over the place. I only say this because the first time we worked together, I made fun of Yasser Arafat, and he went off on a saliva-inducing tirade about how we all misunderstood Yasser. He has since educated me as to the Palestinian way of seeing things, and I have personally adopted the Palestinian position, aside from the hating the Jews part. And I certainly don't do anymore Arafat jokes. Not in front of him, anyway. We're still friends.

When my wife was trying to get pregnant during the in vitro fertilization process, I had to give her several shots every day, mostly Whiskey. We did the in vitro process six times, so I became pretty good at handling a syringe (not that basting a turkey once a year didn't helped). Now, my Palestinian pal has a cousin who is Muslim. She lives in Kuwait, but she was in the States seeing the same fertility specialist as my wife, going through the in vitro process simultaneously with us. While her husband was away on business, she asked if I would administer the shots. As a follower of Jesus, how could I say no? Give a Muslim shots? It is not only my duty as a Christian, but also as an American.

After giving this Muslim woman several shots on a very sensitive area of her body, she has still attended our daughter's last three birthday parties. They visit the States two months every year. So, either she bares no ill will toward me or she really likes cake. But who knows? Maybe it was the whiskey.

One of the most common objections to the supremacy of Christ is, "When you feel that your religion is superior to another religion, doesn't that make you feel like you're superior to these other practitioners?" Not necessarily. Many Christians feel superior because they are nicer looking and much richer, not simply because they have the best religion. (That's irony for those of you who are unfamiliar with it.) The Christian teaching on how to treat people of other faiths is as follows: Love your neighbor as yourself. Jesus made it clear that our neighbor is anyone we come in contact with on our journey through life. The apostle Paul said to "treat everyone with gentleness and respect." So, this would exclude blowing people up. (Hey, here's a little hint for you, if your pastor is wearing fatigues, find a new church.) Moses wrote that God "shows no partiality" to people. That's why I try to make fun of everyone. It's the Christian thing to do.

Treating someone with kindness and respect doesn't mean you have to agree with their belief system or see all belief systems as equally valid to do so. Why does this even need to be said? Well, it doesn't. It can be typed, which I elected to do here.

Of all the issues people find most repugnant about Christianity, it's this idea that Jesus is the only way to God. This is seen as narrow, which is quite insightful really, because Jesus said, "Narrow is the road to life and few are those who find it. But wide is the road to destruction and there's never any construction." (Paraphrase added.)

Randy Newman (the Christian campus radical, not the composer of "Short People" and other songs), while on the panel of his university's seminar on Conflict Analysis and Resolution, heard a Buddhist chaplain say, "Whenever I put up a poster about some Buddhist activity on campus, no one gets upset. Every time an evangelical group puts up a poster, it gets torn down, or people tell the university to stop them. I don't think Christians are doing anything wrong. I just think the nature of their message makes some people hostile."[7]

So, the Christian message is offensive by nature, especially by television. Still, let's try to avoid adding to the offense with our hairdos, if that is even possible. It's that old "I love Jesus, but I hate His followers" syndrome. It may be that people hate the message because the message and the messenger are basically the same. Hey, Christian, you *are* the message. You're the living gospel. The way God revealed Himself in Christ, Christ wants to reveal Himself through you. (Yeah, I know baby boomers don't like responsibility, but that's the way it is, guys.) Christians often say, "They're not rejecting me; they're rejecting Jesus." No, they're rejecting you. Maybe they're rejecting Jesus because of you.

Maybe.

Maybe it's the nature of the message.

If you're one of those people who feel that it's unreasonable to believe that Jesus is the only way to God, I understand exactly how you feel. You feel like 80 million people in the United States alone, who identify themselves as born-again Christians, are wrong. You feel confident that a very large number of people are wrong about Jesus being the only means of salvation. That's exactly how I feel. Except reversed. I feel that large masses of people are wrong about Jesus *not* being the only way to God.

---

7. *Questioning Evangelism: Engaging People's Hearts the Way Jesus Did* by Randy Newman is a great book for people who actually care about that sort of thing (Grand Rapids, MI: Kregel Publications, 2004).

You see? We're more alike than you realize.

In Matthew 11:25, it says, "You have hidden these things from the wise and learned, and revealed them to little children." In other words, morons know better than we do.

The thing that makes Jesus completely unique compared to other religious founders such as Buddha and Muhammad is that He created them. This is a pretty major point. Jesus is the Founder of the founders. Jesus didn't just found Christianity; He founded the entire universe and everyone in it. While Buddha and Muhammad may have said some wonderful things, they didn't create any planets. As Creator, Jesus gets to make the rules. That's the Christian idea of Jesus. He is the Truth. It all emanates from Him. He defines it. He is God walking around among us. He's not just a man like those other guys, even though they wore robes too, which is a God-like thing to do unless you've just gotten out of the shower.

Man, do people hate that.

I saw a nationally known author and speaker who I dearly love. This person is always thought-provoking and intelligent, which is why he often makes me feel so dumb. During his talk before 5,000 youth workers, he explained that "according to an actual study" (as opposed to the ones that speakers just make up to bolster their points), the three most feared groups in America are, in order:

1. Serial killers
2. Pedophiles
3. Evangelical Christians

Now, I can buy the fact that we're feared. Christophobia is rampant for many legitimate reasons, such as the fact that many Christians own and drive Volkswagens just like Ted Bundy. Plus, at our Christmas Eve services, we pour burning wax on people via little candles.

This speaker also said that we're not nice enough. We always seem to be mad at people. We want to separate ourselves into holy huddles or surround flagpoles at public schools to pray, etc. Now, I think there's truth to all that, though I see no harm in surrounding flagpoles and praying to freak out other teenagers. But . . . I think one of the main reasons people fear evangelical Christians is because the gospel is offensive. Christ is the only way to God. It's offensive. Telling people they're sinners is not the offensive part. Everyone will admit they're not perfect. Most people will admit that they have sinned. Some will even own up to the fact that they, too, own a Volkswagen Beetle. Many people will even admit that they need a Savior. It's this supremacy of the Cross of Christ where they begin to hedge.

A nice lady once said to me, "Christians tell everyone that they should believe the way they do, but I think everyone is entitled to believe whatever they want."

I said, "If everyone's entitled to believe whatever they want, then shouldn't people be allowed to believe that they can tell other people what to believe?"

Her mouth dropped open in the most humorous fashion. Really. I have it on tape.

Now, I could quote other theologians (still hopeful about getting that honorary doctorate) about the uniqueness of Christ and His unprecedented influence in this world, but there is something that displays Jesus as the Truth more forcefully than book learnin'. I'll tell you why I believe that Jesus is the only means of salvation.

It's because of my neighbor.

My neighbor is a Christian, and she loves Jesus like she knows Him personally. She didn't just realize one day that she had a felt need and the local Christian church could fill it, not that she wouldn't appreciate a Starbucks before a longwinded sermon. She didn't think it was time that her kids learned some morals, and the local church was responsible to teach them how to act like a holy terror via the youth group. Her newborn infant had cancer, and she needed a real God, *a God who is there.*[8] She didn't need a new kind of Christian. She needed an old kind of God, the miraculous kind. Her newborn son was given no hope to live out the week, and she thought God could help.

At the time, she didn't know toward which version of God to turn. That's why theology is so important. It forms our view of God. If our view of God is skewed, everything else will be off. She spoke with anybody who had a version to share.

Jehovah's Witnesses, come on in.

Mormon elders, please drop by.

Scientologists, well, I can't afford you.

She sincerely spoke with everyone. She was being what some people call open-minded. But always remember that being open-minded is a dangerous thing—that's how she became a Christian.

While in the hospital, there was a nurse's aide who would bring his guitar and play it for her baby, Jacob. Kind of an evangelical singing nun. She didn't know the aide was playing worship songs (that's how well we've disguised them), but it's the only thing that put little Jacob to sleep. My neighbor Jamie started asking questions.

Soon, she claimed to have met this dead guy who brought life. He was dead, now He's alive and not only brings life, but He is Life. Then she started praying to this Jesus, and little baby Jacob is now nine-years-old and lives life full throttle, which, incidentally, is also the volume level of his voice, having a set of lungs that can rival the decibel of any jet engine. I think chemo destroyed his indoor voice.

The doctors don't know why he's alive, but Jamie does.

---

8. A Francis Schaeffer phrase that is still cool but not quoted as often anymore by the new cool Christians.

(I'll leave an open space for you to cry in, if you like.)

Cry here.

At one time, this evangelical singing nurse's aide had a friend who introduced him to Jesus, and before that, his friend had someone who introduced him to Jesus, and so on, going back years and years to the first followers of Jesus, the ones who knew Christ while He was alive, and then dead, and then alive again. It's like that very touching Christmas Eve service where we all light each other's little candles and sometimes start a fire if the lady standing next to us is wearing a flammable jacket with a flowered print.

They told other people who told other people.

I just happen to believe they're all telling the truth, my neighbor and her friends and their friends, and on and on for years and years back to those twelve original followers of Christ.

I believe they've all met the risen Christ.

And some have the candle burns to prove it.

That's really the unity of the holy and catholic church, aside from the Reformation and a myriad of denominational distinctions and church splits. The vein to follow is all these people across the spectrum who still claim they know Jesus alive again. You will find a unity when you listen to their stories about meeting Christ. If you speak with anyone who has undergone a Christian conversion, there's a striking similarity, however varied the details, to each of our stories, starting with our stints as heroin-addicted satanic high priests who are left for dead, join the Army and then pray in a broom closet.

It's such a common tale.

Seriously though, each convert has encountered a very specific spiritual presence that they recognize as the Person of Christ, specifically the Christ as described in the Gospels. This sometimes-dramatic conversion experience (as evidenced by our former lives as satanic high priests) is not typical of any of the other world religions. It's one of the most compelling things about Jesus Christ—that He forgives our sin and somehow we know it in the very core of our souls. Christ forgives sin. He alone. That's really the key. That's what's offensive. Ask Buddha to forgive your sins and see what happens. Ask Muhammad. Ask Krishna. The results will not be the same. Primarily because they are dead.

Christ is alive.

That's why He alone can hear you.

An important point to remember is that though His role as the only Savior of humanity is completely exclusive, His invitation to be that Savior is completely inclusive, with a promise that He will turn away no one who comes to Him.

Look, as I said before, I like Buddha. I think Christians can read Buddha and find many helpful things. I think Buddha was a completely sincere human being. I have some real issues with him abandoning his family, but for the most part, I believe his followers to be thoughtful, sincere people who are concerned about others and excel at miniature golf.

That's the issue for me, though—not the followers, but the founder. You can raise grave and serious doubts about any other founder of a world religion except Jesus Christ. No one says anything bad about Jesus. Sure, lots of Christians suck. That's a given. Wheat and tares. But Jesus is cool. Everyone admits that. Author Michael Green asks, "Where can you find in the teaching of Jesus anything that strikes you as wrong?"[9]

Jesus Christ is the most influential figure who ever lived, religious or otherwise. This is why using the name of Jesus as a curse word is so interesting to me. Years ago, during the sixties' Jesus Movement, singer Barry McGuire said that no one does that with any other religious leader; no one uses their name as

9. Michael Green, *But Don't All Religions Lead to God?* (Grand Rapids, MI: Baker Books, 2002), p. 31.

a curse word. You don't stub your toe and yell, "Ah, Buddha!"[10]
He also noted, "Even the Jewish people, they don't say, 'Abraham! Isaac!'" He then proposed this as a possible strategy of
the devil to diminish the Name that is above all Names by making it a common expression of annoyance. McGuire said, "It's
because his is the only name by which man can be saved. And,
you know, the enemy, Satan, the father of lies, he knows that's
true. And he's tried to make the name of Jesus the most useless,
the most valueless word in our language, spoken hundreds of
times every day and people don't even know what's coming out
of their own mouth."[11]

There's a new idea circulating through the Church about
how to get around the supremacy of Christ. Let's call it an emerging idea. The idea is that Jesus transcends Christianity, meaning
that He reaches Christians through Christianity; but with His
grace He reaches Muslims through Islam and Buddhists through
Buddha, etc. Isn't that a wonderful thought? Did I say wonderful? I meant stupid. First of all, this is a very naive view of Islam,
which is a religion that offers no grace. Second, it's theologically
problematic. If God in Christ is so graciously working through
other religions, then why is God in the Old Testament rather irritated by the idol worship that not only surrounded Israel, but that
was also taking place in Israel? If God can work through other
religions, then why not work through these idols?

It's not that you deny any good that has come from the other
religions of the world; but as a Christian, it is not only remiss, but
it is also downright belittling to a Savior who suffered and died
on a cross for our sins when His followers tiptoe around the issue
of His supremacy. Let's not belittle the pain and sacrifice that

---

10. My good friend comedian Daren Streblow also noticed this independently of
Barry McGuire, as great minds often think alike (and I may have just insulted one
of them).

11. Barry McGuire, *To the Bride*, Myrrh Records, 1975.

Christ experienced on the cross by being too awfully magnanimous toward other religions. If you cannot find the risen Christ in the context of these religions, then they are keeping people from Christ, more so than an obnoxious comedian.

But the most amazing thing, the thing that Jamie learned, is that when you call out to Jesus, when you speak His name from your lips with a cry for help, something happens.

Something real.

Something genuine.

Something good.

Something true.

Jesus, I have been a fool.

It comes as a surprise to most of us that we have been fools.

So laughter, then, is the beginning of prayer.

CHAPTER 8

How to Acquire a Death Threat

(The Bill Maher Theological Approach)

There's a common saying in the comedy world: "It's a comedian's job to say what everyone else is thinking but is afraid to say." In other words, comedy should have some guts (or as much guts as a Christian publisher will allow). Comedy is based on criticism, for the most part, and the following chapter is a critique of world religions and their leaders, all the while lampooning the more blatant flaws of my own. So, much like comedian and social commentator Bill Maher, it's going to sound one-sided and a little mean, though that is certainly not my intention—most of the time. If I were reading this aloud, be assured that it would be with a syrupy-sweet voice, like the one used during that part of a sermon when we want you to know that we sincerely care, if not about you, at least about the tone of our voices.

So let's talk about world religions like the rebel comedians of the 1960s, because there's this idea in our society that you can't make fun of religion. It's a very state correctional facility state of mind.[1]

My first events as a comedian in the Christian realm were in prisons. Progressively, I went from bars to clubs to prisons.

---

1. Gerald Nachman, *Seriously Funny: The Rebel Comedians of the 1950s and 1960s* (New York: Random House, 2003).

And this is how God prepares you for youth events. The Chino State Correctional Facility in Chino, California, was my very first time inside. The first time you go inside, they give you an orientation explaining that you shouldn't refer to the prisoners as inmates or prisoners, but as residents. And you shouldn't call them prisons, but facilities. I'm not sure what the thinking is behind this. Maybe they're hoping the guys will forget they're in prison and just think they live in some really secure apartments but can't get out of their lease.

Initially, I turned the event down because I'm not streetwise. I'm a suburban comic. I don't have any tattoos, so I barely qualify as Emergent. I have a freckle that resembles a cow, but I don't think a roving 4-H gang from Iowa is that intimidating. I've only been in one fight my entire life, and this dates back to seventh grade. I've never been a fighter, even before I was married. If some guy at a bar wanted to beat up my date, I'd be like, "Well, honey, you shouldn't have bumped him." Most bank tellers can kick my butt. What chance do I have in prison telling jokes about toy manufacturers and beauty colleges? I didn't think I'd have anything these guys would relate to, but there I was, license in hand, pants around ankles, being checked into the Chino State Correctional Facility and Center of Orange Jumpsuits by some lady I would never dare call a chick, even though I've been to prison and met the bikers who coined the phrase.

Then came the rules.

Don't ask anyone what they're in for. It's a rule. There's a reason for it. After you find out what they're in for, you might treat them differently. They don't want you hurting the feelings of any convicted thugs. Still, there's compassion behind the rule.

Don't say anything negative about any other religion or religious group. It's a strict rule in prison ministry. You walk inside a prison, even as a volunteer, and you lose some rights. The separation of satire and state.

Now, I'm not advocating rudeness. It's never a good idea to address someone's false beliefs by stating, "You're nuts for believing that." It's best to lovingly relate to people by saying something like, "I understand why you would believe that, because there was a time in my life when I was nuts, too."

I know this is touchy stuff. Many feel that critiquing another person's religion is a bit like correcting your neighbor's children. However, most parents will agree that there are consequences of behavior. That's why I think it's okay to spank other people's children. If you're walking through the mall and see some child acting the brat, give him a little finger-snap on the noggin. Then his parents can say, "You see what happens when you act this way in public? Strangers spank you."

So, don't be offended now that I'm going to spank your religion. Mine misbehaves all the time and I'm the first one to get out that paint stick. (Actually, I never use a paint stick on my daughter, but timeouts don't work with large evangelical churches.)

We don't hesitate to give friends and strangers our opinions on the latest movie release or album or book. Why so hesitant to give our opinions on spiritual issues? If we discuss movies and tripe so freely, why not discuss God? We need to be free to discuss spiritual ideas in the marketplace, criticism included. But, hey, don't take my word for it. Listen to that Darwinian fundamentalist and hater of religion Richard Dawkins, who said, "In any other field, you can argue about politics, taste in music, poetry. There's never the feeling that you're supposed to tiptoe away. You're just not allowed to criticize someone's belief if it's a religious belief, though you're perfectly allowed if it's about politics. I would like to raise people's consciousness against this feeling that religion deserves respect simply because it *is* religion."[2]

---

2. Richard Dawkins, quoted in Laura Sheahen, "Religion: For Dummies," Beliefnet.com, October 17, 2005. http://www.beliefnet.com/story/136/story_13688_1.html.

Hear, hear, jolly ho and whatever else conveys complete agreement with a statement, other than the fact that I have yet in my life to have a heated debate about poetry, besides the short "poetry sucks/no it doesn't" exchange.

Still, I like this Dawkins guy. I think we could be friends.

We discuss everything else.

Why not religion?

Richard and I want to know.

Most of us follow this quaint societal rule that says you're not supposed to talk about politics, religion or the time you accidentally saw your grandma naked. (And let me just state for the record that once you see your grandma naked, those cookies never quite taste the same.)

In his book *The End of Faith*, Sam Harris basically says the same thing as Richard Dawkins: "Criticizing a person's faith is currently taboo in every corner of our culture. On this subject, liberals and conservatives have reached a consensus: religious beliefs are simply beyond the scope of rational discourse."[3] Just be thankful they are not beyond the scope of satire.

Personally, I think challenges are good for *any* religion. If your god can't stand up to a few jokes, just how small is your god? Dashboard deities need not apply. Don't you want a God with some guts? (Muslims need not answer.)

Harvard professor of psychiatry Dr. Armand M. Nicholi, Jr., wrote, "None of us can tolerate the notion that our worldview may be based on a false premise and, thus, our whole life headed in the wrong direction."[4] And that's *really* what we're intolerant of—other people being right.

---

3. Sam Harris, *The End of Faith: Religion, Terror and the Future of Reason* (New York: W. W. Norton and Company, Inc., 2004), p. 13.

4. Armand M. Nicholi, Jr., *The Question of God: C. S. Lewis and Sigmund Freud Debate God Love, Sex and the Meaning of Life* (New York: Simon and Schuster, 2002), p. 6. This is the kind of book that you can't put down. It's tremendous.

I understand the danger of what I'm about to do. Salman Rushdie received death threats from Islamic extremists after writing *The Satanic Verses*. As a matter of fact, Salman Rushdie actually wrote this chapter for me. Pass that along to all of your radical Muslim friends: Salman Rushdie is quite a wisenheimer.

Besides, a comedian who doesn't receive a death threat now and then is just not doing his or her job. (Way to go, Salman.)

As you read this chapter, you will see, through finely crafted comedy (by Salman Rushdie), the major differences between the world's religions.

Enjoy the show.

A Comedian's Guide to World Religion

"The first 450 pages of the Bible is crap."

He said it with gusto but not anger. He was 87 years old and fit as a fiddle, which was probably a hip saying in his day. At 87, he was just happy to have his hips. He was a multimillionaire or a billionaire, or not related to me. He said his gift was making money. I told him my birthday is September 12. My chances of landing some cash in a birthday card are slim since I'm sitting next to him on Southwest Airlines, the Wal-Mart of the skies. He didn't mean to insult me by saying the first 450 pages of the Bible is crap, but, well, it's the crap I've based my life on. So, one of us is an idiot. But what can you say to that without sounding defensive?

"Yeah, I understand. I probably wouldn't believe it myself if I hadn't encountered the risen Christ."[5]

. . . is what I wish I would have said. However, I kept my cool. I spoke kindly to this cheap billionaire who wore steel-toed boots. We discussed religion a little more, specifically

---

5. I picked up this line from L.A. pastor Erwin McManus who has pithy lines for many occasions and people types.

Islam and Christianity; then Mormonism came up somehow. Then he said, "I believe in God. But there are 2,700 different religions. You can't possibly know which one to follow."

Now, I'm not sure where he pulled those figures from— I had my head turned when he reached into his . . . however, if there are 2,700 different religions, then I'd venture to say that 2,695 of them are crap.

There are only 10 basic sitcom plots. There's no way people could invent 2,700 distinctly different religions. Mortimer Adler, in his book *Truth in Religion*, observed "that if you read the sacred texts of the world's religions at face value, only three actually claim that the creator God has revealed himself . . . Judaism, Christianity and Islam."[6] And since Muhammad stole most of his ideas from Judaism and Christianity, that leaves two. (This is only the opinion of some scholars and not necessarily the correct opinion. Please don't hurt me.)

All religions are probably a variation of the big five, which are, from oldest to youngest: Hinduism, though this is disputed by Yezidism, but who takes them seriously anymore; followed by Buddhism, Judaism, Christianity, and Islam. Throw in Zoroastrianism if you want. (Like the Yezidists don't have enough to complain about these days.) Or even Confucius. These are the big dogs. These are the tails worth pulling. Man bites religion.

I will focus my attention on making fun of the dominant world religions,[7] which means there will be no jokes about the prophet Zoroaster. The most disturbing aspect of this whole comparative religions issue, though, is that some religions

---

6. John Burke actually pointed this out in *Listening to the Beliefs of Emerging Churches: Five Perspectives* (Grand Rapids, MI: Zondervan, 2007), p. 60, but it just sounds clunky to quote someone quoting someone.

7. I covered Judaism in chapter 2.

being right is much more frightening than other religions being right. For example, if the Buddha is right, then I've really nothing to worry about as a practicing Christian. As a matter of fact, I can still practice my false religion without a care in the world, other than the fact that Mel Gibson still has working vocal cords. However . . . however . . . if Christianity is true, then Buddhists need to take a second look.

All Elephants Lead to God

The view that all religions are basically the same is just silly. I'm always amazed when someone says, "Yeah, I took a comparative religion course and they're all basically the same."

I want to ask, "Were you not paying attention?"

I want to—but I don't. I'm only bold about my faith in print.

One of the most popular analogies used to demonstrate the theoretical compatibility of world religions is the blind men and the elephant. The analogy goes like this: Four blind men stumble upon an elephant, which often happens when you're blind and trying to find the restroom at the zoo. This is why you should always stay with your tour group. The first man feels the trunk and says it's a snake, but no one puts any stock in what he says because he's dumb enough to pick up a snake. The second man feels the legs and says it's a tree, but no one puts any stock in what he says because he doesn't notice the elephant at the end of the tree trunk. The third man feels the tail and calls out, "Rope." Everyone just rolls his or her eyes, but no one notices. The fourth feels the elephant's side and says, "It's a wall. It's a rather poorly built wall because it bows out right here, but it's a wall alright." Then an employee of the zoo comes along and says, "What are you doing in the elephant's cage? Your group is looking for you." They say, "Who do you think you are?" He says, "Who do you say that I am?"

They ignore him, carry on their examination and soon the elephant sits on the guy pulling at its tail. So, always remember—some religions can crush you.

Even Bertrand Russell, the dead philosopher who wrote *Why I Am Not a Christian,* said in that very book, "It is evident as a matter of logic that, since they (the world religions) disagree, not more than one of them can be true."

He just happened to believe they were all false. But if one is true, it can only be one. Thank you for your clear thinking, Bertrand Russell, wherever you are. (And we hope not there.)

Most people will agree that we can't all be right. That's not to say that other religions haven't contributed to society, note George Harrison and Richard Gere. Okay, note George Harrison. Truth is truth no matter where you find it. That's the issue, though. What is truth? Can you actually find it? Is it beyond our scope? Can we possibly find it among the fish tanks and decorative statues of local Chinese restaurants?

Buddhanity

I read Karen Armstrong's book on Buddha. The paperback version is 187 pages, and I read close to half of it, so this pretty much makes my explanation half-witted. (I would say my explanation is half-*something elsed* if I didn't think so many dear Christian readers would take offense.)

Buddha believed in multiple little gods, which was the cultural norm for his day. These little gods were just people at one time and could easily become plants after a bad year of godding. So, Buddha ignored the little gods because people don't really fear your wrath if you're shorter than they are. Still, he wanted to find a way to achieve this state called nirvana, which basically means that you can abandon your wife and child and not feel guilty about it, which is what Sid did.

(Sid is Buddha's real name—Sid Hartha. Ba-da-bing.)

During Buddha's time, there was a bunch of people living in the forests who wore orange robes and shaved their heads. The only time they came into town was to get free food. They were known as spiritual seekers, but today we call them bums.

Buddha, after naming his little boy "Fetter" and popularizing the spousal nickname "Ball and Chain," decided to join these spiritual seekers and pursue deliverance from suffering, sometimes known as marriage. Buddha (Sid) had to leave home to free himself of desire, which is what most of the forest monks perceived to be the biggest problem with living—desire. It is obvious that the one desire Buddha didn't free himself from is food. This is something Buddhism has in common with American evangelicalism, where you get holiness points for avoiding all kinds of things except food that's really bad for you.

His goal was worthy, the elimination of ego, which makes the popularity of Buddhism in Hollywood surprising. He believed that whatever spiritual state you could attain as a human being, you could attain it naturally without the aid of steroids. So, in Buddhism you don't really need a Buddha. Buddha would probably be very disappointed that Buddhism even exists. The guy who invented this orange robe and shaved head thing is really more of a Buddha than Buddha, because we don't even know who he is—so there's truly the elimination of ego.

Buddhists love the Buddha, which is not what Buddha was going for at all. So, it's sad but true—Buddha failed at Buddhism.

In Buddhism there is no god, but you still get punished, which kind of stinks. Buddhism has a moral law of cause and effect. It's kind of like spiritual banking. You make deposits in your good account; that's like a savings account of your good deeds. When you want to have a fun weekend, you transfer funds from your good account into your bad account and at the end of your life the accounts are balanced. Since Buddhism has no god, I'm not sure who does the accounting, but if you come out in the red, you have to go back to Earth and get in line again at the spiritual ATM. Another thing to watch out for: Sometimes when your account is overdrawn, the Temple will keep your card.

Now, of course, as with all religions there are variations and in-house debates and rivalries, but space does not permit me to delve into the various branches of Buddhism. (I'll have to save that for my next book, *A Comedian's Guide to World Religion*. To publisher: wink, nudge.) For now, this superficial sketch must do.

Like Judaism and Christianity, Buddhism also has seven deadly sins that are, in order of popularity, anger, pride, envy, lust, gluttony, greed and sloth. The Judeo-Christian list of seven deadly sins is according to Proverbs 6: haughty eyes, a lying tongue, murder, a heart that devises wicked schemes, feet that are quick to rush to evil, a false witness who pours out lies, and a man who stirs up dissension among brothers.

Basically, your local church.

Now, in the scheme of things, Buddhism may be true, but it's certainly not the same as Christianity.

Hinduism: Buddhism Without Buddha

Hinduism is often said to be the oldest religion, but only because Noah and his family never made their relationship with God an official religion. This is why patent laws exist today.

Hinduism is a lot like Buddhism, but without the Buddha. Buddhism is basically an outgrowth of Hinduism, a kind of new and improved Hinduism without all those annoying little gods. There are literally millions of gods in Hinduism. *And you thought denominations were a problem?* Hinduism also has this very vague force called Brahman, which helps space cadets in battle or something. Brahman is an impersonal and transcendent force that pervades everything that lives and breathes, and I mean everything. Your cat has Brahman. Your innermost self is identical to Brahman, according to Hinduism. You and your cat's innermost self both have Brahman. This is why cats seem to ignore people. They are contemplating the universe. Dogs don't have Brahman. Dogs are without souls, and that's why it's okay to shoot them when they bark at night.[8]

The idea of Brahman is similar to the concept of God's omnipresence. God's presence pervades everything in life. In Him we live and move and have our cake and eat it too (or so we think these days). We can't take a breath except that God's presence in our world allows it. Everything in life owes its breath to God. Even your pets. This is why cats ignore you. They are dependent upon God.

Dogs have no souls.

While thoroughly researching Hinduism by typing the word "Hinduism" into the little Google box, I discovered that Hinduism "does not have a single founder, a specific theological system, a single system of morality, or a central religious organization."[9] They might believe in one main god with multiple little gods, or just lots of gods. It depends. So, basically, if you have a little statue, a mat and you believe in reincarnation, you can practice Hinduism.

One of the main tenets of Hinduism is reincarnation. Personally, I have come to the conclusion that if reincarnation is true, if I have lived other lives, then I want my stuff back. That's a lot of accumulated real estate, thank you.

---

8. Yes, this is a recurring theme for me, because I am trying to save the lives of dogs by getting their owners to shut them up at night.

9. "Hinduism: The World's Third Largest Religion," www.religioustolerance.org. http://www.religioustolerance.org/hinduism.htm (accessed September 2007).

The transmigration of the soul and what people return to Earth as, much like Buddhism, has to do with "the spiritual bank account." Hinduism calls "the spiritual bank account" karma, allowing really rich people to think they deserve to be really rich because they were so wonderful in a past life. No wonder this is so popular in show business, the elite in a caste society. It's just more accolades. *Good job, man. Way to go. You deserve everything that comes your way.* And if you see a bum starving on the corner, leave him be. He probably deserves it. Who are you to monkey with the law of karma? If you relieve his suffering, how will he ever fulfill his suffering quota?

That is more of a westernized view of Hinduism, though. In more traditional Hinduism, and in Buddhism especially, a compassionate person will rarely escape the circle of life, because they will always return to Earth where their help is needed. They're like mothers who can't take a vacation. Still, in Hinduism and Buddhism, your salvation comes by your own good works, your own righteousness.

Good luck with that.

Now, in the scheme of things, Hinduism may be true, but it's not the same.

"Confucius Say" Is Not Just a Fun Saying

Though many of us actually say, "Confucius say"—most of us don't really know what he said. Confucius thought that people were basically good. Confucius say, "Likewise man's nature is basically good, but can be forced into bad ways through external pressure." I guess he never had any children. They don't need external pressure to be bad; they just need to be left alone for five minutes.

Confucius's ideas were ahead of his time. When the rest of the ancient world was using sundials, he had a clock radio.

Rather than overtly religious, his ideas were more of a social and political nature. Indeed, his thinking was so far advanced that he couldn't get a job with any of the local feudal lords, let alone on the assembly line of the local sundial factory. Just as Jesus said, "A prophet receives no honor in his home town," this was true in Confucius's life too.

None of the original writings of Confucius exist today, because the dynasty at the time censored dissenting viewpoints by killing all the people with viewpoints. This is called *ad hominem* overkill, showing us all once again that the thing that must be avoided in our culture is the suppression of dissenting voices, even if they're the voices of morons. The Klan can stand on one side of the street holding signs that say, "White power." We can stand on the other side holding signs that say, "White power? Tell that to your teeth." Granted, it's also an *ad hominem* argument, but no one dies.

Generally, Confucius said some really good things that completely align with Christianity. He had some great words, just not the ones that lead to salvation. After you get saved, then sure, go ahead and Confute.

I've found one of the greatest problems with Confucianism is that his followers don't know what to call themselves. When you ask them what religion they follow, they don't say, "I'm a Confucian." They can't say, "I'm Confucius." I don't even know if "Confucianist" is a word, because my spell-checker doesn't recognize it. Oddly, my spell-checker recognizes the word "spell-checker," which is not nearly as ancient as the term "Confucianist." That's confucing. (I have to admit, I'm laughing at this third-grade joke. But then again, I host a comedy show called *Bananas, appeeling comedy for the whole family*.) Plus, I don't even know if Confucianists meet regularly. It's really hard to have an organized religion if you don't put an ad in the yellow pages. That right there is really the test of having a major world religion. If your belief system is not advertised in the yellow pages, it's certainly not legitimate.

Fundamentalist Muslims Are More Frightening Than Fundamentalist Christians, and That's a Fact
by Salman Rushdie

The word "Islam" means *submission*, specifically a woman's submission in all things to her husband who is supposed to submit to Allah; but they don't really make a big deal about that part of it. There is no Muslim Promise Keepers.

Muslims, the men anyway, look forward to a paradise of wine, women and song. Their religion is kind of like, "Be good on Earth so you can be bad in heaven."

Islamic women look forward to Islamic men dying.

Muhammad never claimed to be God. He just claimed to be God's main prophet who received all his messages from God through the angel Gabriel. And he may have been mistaken. Rumor has it that the angel Gabriel and Satan look a lot alike.

And that right there is one of the most unpopular answers to the question, "Where do other religions come from?" One answer is that demons disguised as angels gave them to certain humans, but we'll cover Mormonism later. Spin-doctor demons seem completely plausible to me. However, this is not something you want to share during a psychological evaluation.

The other answer to this question, just as plausible but not nearly as titillating, is that men made them up to get women. For example, say your best friend's wife is really attractive, but you continually run into the problem of, well, her being married to your best friend. If you invent a religion that you claim

God gave you and then convince your best friend and his wife of this—you're really only one step away from "God told me to tell you to give me your wife." Some scholars believe that Muhammad invented Islam to get chicks. Or he was speaking to demons disguised as angels. Either/or. That's all reasonable scholarship for a comedian.

This statement will rile some people, but fundamentalist Muslims are much scarier than fundamentalist Christians, because fundamentalist Muslims want their children to die a martyr's death, if by martyr you mean terrorist. Christian fundamentalists are big on dying a martyr's death too, but it has more to do with giving up your life to malaria while trying to make sure all the Yanomamo tribeswomen have blouses on.

In fundamentalist Islam, which is certainly not practiced by all Muslims, especially the ones who enjoy sitcoms, they believe you'll go directly to paradise if you run into an enemy camp with explosives strapped to your underwear. Suddenly, those Pentecostals seem pretty tame, don't they? Okay, so they're shouting and holding up their hands. Doesn't really compare to a bomb in your underwear, now does it? I don't know why I was so upset about that tongues thing.

Let us say, hypothetically, that Islam turns out to be a false religion, just for argument's sake. Think about it, going on a suicide mission for a false religion. That has to be a pretty disappointing death.

Boom!

"Allah?"

"No—Jesus."

"Crap. No virgins?"

"Just My mom."

Ayaan Hirsi Ali, in her incendiary book *Infidel*, writes, "True Islam, as a rigid belief system and moral framework, leads to cruelty."[10] And that's much worse than anything Salman Rushie has written here, so if your anger compels you to cut something, cut him some slack.

If you happen to be a Christian, you understand that the Crusades were not representative of Jesus. Many Muslims feel the same way about 9/11 and other violence done in the name of Allah. It's not representative of the way they practice their faith. Not all Muslims condone the violence done in the name of Islam, but now would be a good time to speak up about it.

Again, in the scheme of things, Islam may be true, but it's not the same.

Foxe's Book of Ferraris: A History of Abundance and Greed in the American Prosperity Gospel

Founder of Scientology, L. Ron Hubbard once said that if you want to become filthy rich, you should start a religion. This is something Scientology has in common with the Prosperity Movement of American-brand Christianity where believers like to encourage greedy, overtly materialistic preachers by giving them more money for their ministries, which consist of asking for more money for their ministries. They've confused faith with begging. Hey, if these preachers all have that much faith, you think they could just pray all that money in rather than beg for it?

I believe that God provides miraculously, but if you think God *must* provide for you because of your tithes and offerings, all you've done is reduced God into a manageable idol for your own private use. The Church of Cha-Ching. Christianity as a pyramid scheme.

---

10. Ayaan Hirsi Ali, *Infidel* (New York: Simon and Schuster, 2007), p. 272.

What kind of gospel is that?
Would you like to give your heart to Jesus?
Not really.
What if there's a Rolls Royce involved?
Well, sure.
And for only 10 percent of your yearly income, God can make you a millionaire.
Really?
If you believe.
What happens if my faith is weak?
Do you want your Rolls repoed?
No.
Then believe.
It's that easy?
It is if you don't want to get cancer and die.

What many professing Christians fail to realize is that the abundant life according to the apostle Paul can mean an abundance of beatings, imprisonments and hardships (see 2 Tim. 3:12). Did you get your blessing yet?

The thing that brings God the most glory is when people in hardship and persecution trust Him because they believe so strongly in His character. This is why there is something called *Foxe's Book of Martyrs* and not *Foxe's Book of Ferraris*. Jesus doesn't want you to follow Him because He can line your pocket book or remove your bunions or fill your garage with fancy cars (or your hut with multiple pigs if you're a Third Worlder). He wants you to follow Him because He's the Truth.

As Darius Dunson (aka Guadscent) told Lauren Sandler in her book *Righteous*, "The biggest enemy to Christianity is the misrepresentation of Christianity."[11]

---

11. Lauren Sandler, *Righteous: Dispatches from the Evangelical Youth Movment* (New York: Viking, 2006) p. 152.

Answering Objections
(Like It Will Make a Difference)

The biggest objection people will have about this chapter is, "It's not very Christian to talk negatively about people's religious beliefs." Really? You know what Jesus said to some of the religious leaders of His day? He called them hypocrites to their faces and "white washed tombs full of dead men's bones." That's what I love about Jesus—He's not very Christian.

When the apostle Paul, in the midst of his "Have I Got News for You" tour, entered the city of Athens (see Acts 17), which was a cultural Mecca of higher learning and religious diversity (basically the Des Moines, Iowa, of its day), he was "greatly distressed to see that the city was full of idols."[12] After a heated exchange with some Epicurean and Stoic philosophers (by today's standards imagine Paul debating Hugh Hefner and Lieutenant Commander Spock simultaneously), Paul was taken to a meeting of the Areopagus, which was a council of the city's political and philosophical elders—basically the Des Moines, Iowa, of its day. Before you could go about spouting your ideas, you had to pass muster with these elders.

Paul says several things to them. First, he begins by telling them, "Nice robes," and he doesn't say it sarcastically as would be expected. Then he tells them where they're getting it right. He doesn't just tell them their religions are patently false, which is not what I am contending here either concerning the world

---

12. In downtown San Jose, California, the city spent half a million dollars for a sculpture of an ancient Mexican idol called Quetzalcoatl that actually looks like a gargantuan dog turd, certainly symbolic of misspent funds. They erected this sculpture to pay homage to the city's Mexican heritage, even though the number of Hispanics who still worship this idol are dwindling by the day. "People of San Jose! I see that in every way you are very religious. For as I walked around your downtown, I noticed the colossal dog poop-looking idol of Quetzalcoatl. That you may no longer worship crap, I will proclaim the unknown God to you" (Acts 17:23, author's parody).

religions, off-brand cults or burgeoning new religions like Wal-Mart. Paul then quotes their religious poets, who basically say that we are all children of God because God created us, the same thing most science teachers in Kansas are saying today. Then, he tells them that in the past, God overlooked their ignorance. But now, he says, God "commands all people everywhere to repent."

Sure, Paul uses common ground as a starting point, but let us not forget the other things he mentions about their religious perspective, such as the fact that it's based on ignorance. Gerald R. McDermott writes that Paul "corrected a host of religious notions which no doubt were held by some Athenians: that God lives in temples, could be served by human hands, is distant, is like gold or silver or stone, and can be represented by an artistic image."[13]

In the Hebrew Bible, when Elijah challenges the religions of Baal and Asherah, he says to their prophets, after their gods are a no-show, "Shout louder! Perhaps he is deep in thought or busy or traveling" (1 Kings 18:27). I do most of my deep thinking on the can. I think Elijah was basically saying, "Maybe your god had to go potty." But then again, I don't read Hebrew.

Don't misunderstand my sentiments in this chapter, unless you're one of those rare souls who gets irony. In no way am I arguing that Christians are better than practitioners of other religions. If one is a follower of Jesus, you can truly weep over the atrocities committed in the name of Christ by Christian idiots. I'm not saying that Christians are better, but I am saying that Jesus is better. These two chapters promote the idea that My God Is Bigger Than Your god, not My People of Faith Are Better Than Your People of Faith.

It begins and ends with Christ.

---

13. Gerald R. McDermott, *God's Rivals: Why Has God Allowed Different Religions? Insights from the Bible and the Early Church* (Downers Grove, IL: InterVarsity Press, 2007), p. 81.

Ayaan Hirshi Ali writes in the introduction to her book, "There are some things that must be said, and there are times when silence is an accomplice to injustice."[14] Following her lead, I wrote this chapter because we Emergent types are too silent concerning this subject, confusing "names" with "sticks and stones."

The gospel is not polite.

It is demanding.

"Repent and believe" is not an invitation.

In some parts of the world, you can't speak freely because they actually throw sticks and stones. In America we just call you names, tell people you were stoned and hope it sticks.

I enjoyed Ayaan's book *Infidel* very much, even though surprisingly, in the end, she ends up an infidel.[15] She writes, "Essentially, I needed to be convinced that Islam was *true*. And it was beginning to dawn on me that although many wonderful people were sure it was true, there seemed to be breakdowns in its consistency."[16]

She wanted truth.

How very un-postmodern of her.

There are still people out there who want to be convinced that Christianity is true. That's why I rarely leave the house. Who needs that kind of pressure?

If nothing else, consider this chapter one small font forward in the affirmation of freedom of speech. Consider it the cartoon of Muhammed that most American newspapers were

---

14. Ali, *Infidel*, p. xii.

15. This is completely understandable, though, because she went from a Middle Ages mindset and jumped right into an Enlightenment mindset, which is certainly far superior to her former worldview but, unfortunately, this blinded her to the shortcomings of modernistic thought, which of course means now she's Dutch.

16. Ali, *Infidel*, p. 272.

afraid to publish. It really was rather perplexing to figure out what all the fuss about that cartoon was, since we never did get to see it. Maybe we would empathize with the offended religion after seeing the cartoon and think to ourselves, "Sure, I'd riot, too." Who knows? We riot for lesser things in America, like sporting events. And this is an important point to remember. So, the next time you see news footage of Muslims in the streets firing weapons, cheering and beating themselves with sticks, just imagine they're at a football game, and they won't seem so nuts.

According to Christian theology, what people believe is of vital importance. Our entire belief system is based on faith alone. Faith in Christ, what He did, why He did it. It's a faith that saves, justifies us before God instead of our own righteousness. "They being ignorant of God's righteousness, and seeking to establish their own righteousness, have not submitted to the righteousness of God. For Christ is the end of the law for righteousness to everyone who believes" (Rom. 10:3-4). You see how important believing the right things about God is? It's the difference between self-righteousness and true grace. It's the difference between false beliefs and the truth. "The visions of your prophets were false and worthless; they did not expose your sin to ward off your captivity. The oracles they gave you were misleading" (Lam. 2:14). God cares about what people are being taught.

I understand that these are emotionally charged issues, and that's why it's rather disappointing that I can't be there to witness what has probably become a throbbing vein in your forehead.

So, what does God think of those who follow other religions? The verse below is about a tribe that had left God and gone astray. I think it speaks His heart for every missing child, whatever faith tradition they find themselves in:

"Is not Ephraim my dear son,
the child in whom I delight?
Though I often speak against him,
I still remember him.
Therefore my heart yearns for him;
I have great compassion for him,"
declares the Lord.
(Jer. 31:20)

I understand that many of you will find this chapter disconcerting, some will even find it intolerant, and I assure you I will mention your feelings to Salman Rushdie, the author who ghostwrote this chapter for me, whose name and address I can supply upon request, if you will do me the small courtesy of remembering my cooperation. I begged him to tone things down, but he would have none of it.

He wanted truth.

Sorry, Muhammad.

CHAPTER 9

Damn Theology

(Why Hell Is a Good Idea)

Personally, I think hell is a good idea, but the real question is: Can you write about hell and be funny at the same time? Well, Dante wrote a book about hell called *The Divine Comedy*, which is about one man's journey to hell (as far as I can tell), and really isn't all that funny. It's kind of a misleading title actually. So, in answer to the question, Can you write about hell and be funny?, the answer is, "Well, not if you're Dante." I think it's a great title, but it's not another theological humor book, as you would expect.

Shakespeare wrote, "Hell hath no fury like a woman scorned." Now, what we learn from Shakespeare is that bad relationships can make you an excellent writer.[1]

The other day, as far as you know, I heard someone use the phrase "come hell or high water." I'm not sure that I understand the idea behind that saying. In hell you suffer, in high water you drown. It's sounds like a lose-lose proposition to me. Who came up with that? Probably some guy stuck between a rock and a hard place.

Some people claim to have been to hell and back, but it turns out they were only in Newark, New Jersey. I have been stranded for six hours at the Newark International Airport, and coincidentally, I am reading Brian McLaren's book on hell. He

---

1. Comedy is a bad relationship seen from a distance.

wrote an entire book on hell. My entire book is not about hell; it just seems that way when you're reading it.

Hell is a concept that many people stridently reject because it makes sinning less fun. So, if you're in the middle of some gross sinning, I must apologize for putting a damper on it with this chapter.

Since I am trapped in hell and find it not only a reality but also part of the 2,000-year-old tradition of Christianity, I will make fun of Brian's theology by using his own method of creative nonfiction.

Here's my Socratic dialogue on the subject:

"How can you believe in hell? I thought God was supposed to be good?"

"God is good. That's why hell's a good idea. Because God thought of it."

Okay, it's pop apologetics, but why does hell get such a bad rap these days? Why should heavy metal have all the good songs about hell? What about rap?

As you can probably tell, I will defend the traditional view of hell that is less beta male friendly. As a matter of fact, you might say that I'm going to be raising hell. *Tee-hee. Hand over mouth.* I hope it becomes popular again because it's certainly consistent with God's holiness; yet many pastors today want to shut the hell up about hell, renting out its space in the Bible to Starbucks. "If your right eye causes you to sin, gouge it out and throw it away. It is better for you to lose one part of your body than for your whole body to be thrown into Starbucks" (see Matt. 5:29).

Not quite as effective.

It's argued by many Emergent Church leaders[2] that hell is not an effective way to get people's attention anymore. This is

---

2. Look, I can't name them all because that would mean thumbing through more books. Besides, hitchhiking is dangerous.

why churches now hire comedians. Chances of gaining an unbeliever's serious attention by trying to scare him or her with
threats of hell are about as good as . . . well, a snowball's chance
in hell. I agree that hell has lost some oomph, but only because
no one believes in it anymore. When people believe in hell, it's
really effective.[3] Just take a moment and think about eternal
torment. Try that at your next church service: "We're going to
pause now and have a moment of silence while we think about
eternal torment." Pause . . . two, three, four. "Will the ushers
come forward, please?"

The issue of hell divides Christians into five separate theological camps: (1) people who believe in hell as a place of eternal suffering; (2) people who believe in hell, but believe the
residents will be annihilated at some point; (3) people who believe there may be hope after hell; (4) people who have an easier
time cheating on their spouses (basically everyone in the previ-
ous group); (5) people who believe that everyone will be saved
from hell (people who cheat on their spouses *and* their taxes).

Here are five views of hell without their various levels and
villas, though all include free parking. The question is, Which
view is more biblically accurate? Well, the one I believe, of course.
Read on to see if you're as biblical as me.

The Traditional View: Monsters, Inc.

The traditional view of hell is that it's a final dumping ground
for sin[4] and a never-ending place of some type of torment, kind
of like a spiritual DMV, but while you're standing in line you
periodically get poked in the butt with a pitchfork. (It's about
hell. I had to work in a pitchfork joke. Union rules.)

---

3. Jonathan Edwards had an advantage in that his congregation actually believed in
   hell. The other advantage to his preaching is that *he* actually believed in hell, too.

4. I think Dallas Willard referred to hell this way. If not, then I take all the credit.

Even within Orthodoxy (the group of people who are right), there are various views of hell (four, according to one book I read, cleverly titled *Four Views on Hell*).[5]

The first view is called the literal view. This guy takes hell literally, meaning that if he tells you to go there, then find a manhole marked "hell," remove it and jump in. He believes that you're going to burn in actual fire, which will be much worse than a woman scorned who only key scratches your car.

The next orthodox view is the metaphorical view. This guy thinks that hell is real and it's really bad, but eternal fire is just a way to describe it because not everyone dates the same people. This guy has had better luck with relationships. He believes that however bad hell is, it's as bad as burning in fire forever, but only nearly as frightening as a woman scorned.

I think that saying "It's a lake of fire or the equivalent thereof" is more biblically accurate. But then again, I haven't dumped anyone lately. However, I have been married 14 years and, thankfully, have avoided scorning my wife.

Brian McLaren dedicates his book on hell to people who "have been repulsed by ugly, unworthy images of a cruel, capricious, merciless, tyrannical deity." I dedicated my book to my wife and daughter, two people who don't find me repulsive. According to Brian, if you haven't been repulsed by the traditional view of hell, well—you suck, because you're not one of the people who are repulsed. You're obviously less compassionate, and definitely less merciful, because you're probably as cold and mean and cruel as your view of God. No wonder you vote Republican.[6] (Cheap joke. Too easy. Couldn't resist. My apologies.)

---

5. John Walvoord, William Crockett, Zachary Hayes and Clark Pinnock, *Four Views on Hell* (Grand Rapids, MI: Zondervan, 1996).

6. I'm gonna keep harping on this point throughout the book, but we should never align Jesus with ANY political party. Read *The Myth of a Christian Nation* by Gregory Boyd if you need good reasons (Grand Rapids, MI: Zondervan, 2007).

Brian says that if the traditional view of hell is even remotely correct, then God is a monster. And if God is not a monster, then you are a monster for believing it.[7] I think that's kind of mean of him. (Stop being such a conservative, Brian.) Look, if we all end up in heaven, it doesn't really matter if we're monsters or not, now does it?

One of the reasons that many people believe in hell is because they have dated me. That's beside the point. People believe in hell because we *are* monsters.

Annihilation: The Ouch and Poof View

There is a heterodox view of hell called annihilation, meaning that God will punish you for a time, just to make a point, and then obliterate you, so you won't remember His point. Thus, ouch and poof—you will no longer exist. Annihilationists have a hard time making their position as scary as the traditional ones, because according to their view, God is saying, "I'm going to teach you a lesson that you will soon forget."

Okay. Whatever.

Universalism: Hell with Air-Conditioning

Brian might believe in hell, but it's an air-conditioned hell.[8] He suggests that hell may not be the last word. There might be a word after that, which is good news for anyone who has a heart attack and dies while committing adultery.

This view basically amounts to universalism, the belief that everyone will one day prefer Universal Studios to Disneyland.

---

7. Brian McLaren, *The Last Word and the Word After That: A Tale of Faith, Doubt and a New Kind of Christianity* (San Francisco: Jossey-Bass, 2005), p. 40.

8. Christopher W. Morgan and Robert A. Peterson, eds., *Hell Under Fire: Modern Scholarship Reinvents Eternal Punishment* (Grand Rapids, MI: Zondervan, 2004), p. 40.

That's as ridiculous as the other definition of universalism, which says everyone will eventually be saved from hell.

Brian says that "universalism is not as bankrupt of biblical support as some suggest."[9] Then he lists a bunch of Bible verses in support of universalism. So, I looked up all 13 verses he referenced and I was quite surprised after reading them and must confess that universalism is as bankrupt as ever.

One of the verses he uses to buttress universalism is 1 Peter 3:9, which says, "He [God] is patient with you, not wanting anyone to perish, but everyone to come to repentance." It is true that God doesn't want anyone to perish, and this is why you should even be kind to your mother-in-law. But if you don't repent, how can He save you against your will? It would put God in the unfortunate position of justifying the sin of the unrepentant if He saved them. God is not your grandma. All 13 verses Brian lists have to be placed on a taffy machine to build a case for universalism. (You have to stretch them.)

However, the greatest drawback to universalism is this: Where do Universalists tell someone to go when they're really upset with him?

"Why don't you just go to . . . ah, I guess I'll see you later."

Brian writes, "It has been said that anyone who is not a Universalist should be at the very least a Universalist sympathizer."[10] Really? Well, it's also been said that there's no greater stupidity than a stupid intellectual. People who believe in justice and grace and righteousness and truth should be at the very least a damnation sympathizer, because promoting the idea that hell might not be the last word after you die is good news for horses' patooties. That's good news for parents who sucked at it; for dad's who deserted their families and moms who

9. McLaren, *The Last Word and the Word After That*, p. 103.

10. Ibid., p. 183.

didn't protect their children; for the pirates of the Caribbean and the pirates of Wall Street; for Hitler and Stalin and Vlad the Impaler. There's hope for you yet, Charles Manson. (Actually, there is, because he's still alive. Grace is the good news for the above categories of people, not the elimination of hell.)

Brian says that this view of hell in no way promotes the idea that all religions are equal.[11] If we all end up in the same place eventually, I'd say that's quite an equalizer. It makes hell irrelevant.

Losing Hell: *Why Is Hell Important?*
Question Submitted by MOPS, Mothers of Preschoolers

The removal of hell lightens our view of sin, since we don't have to worry about going there when we die. You might as well publish a Bible called *Good News for Internet Porn Kings*. The work of Christ is only good news when you embrace His death and resurrection. It's a work that changes the hearts of people, lessening sin in the lives of men and women and the Internet sites they visit. Apparently, the damage that sin causes is so extensive that it deserves a hell. And this is why you can never be friends with your ex-girlfriends.[12] It's unpleasant to spend time with someone who is only happy when you're being tormented. Unfortunately, this is how many people view God in light of hell.

This is one of the questions Brian asks in his book: "How could a view of hell be seen as flowing from the love of God?"[13] Easy. Because God loves holiness and justice and righteousness and truth and goodness and etc. (We can only imagine that God loves the abbreviation etc., because He is infinite.)

---

11. Ibid.

12. Can also be applied to ex-boyfriends, of course.

13. McLaren, *The Last Word*, p. 188.

Hell makes a distinction between righteousness and un-righteousness, between justice and oppression, between gracious help and exploitation, between what God loves and what God hates. Take away hell and God is no longer holy, repentance no longer matters and Calvary becomes a sham. Take away hell and we lose all our famous scary sermons. *"Sinners in the Hands of a Permissive God"*?

Albert Mohler makes a great point, one that more churches need to place on their reader board signs, when he writes, "God's love has been redefined so that it is no longer holy."[14]

Remove the doctrine of hell and Christianity soon becomes a religion of "what's the point?" Brian's book on hell seems to be an adventure in missing the point.[15] *Tee-hee. Hand over mouth.*

Now, I understand that people will harp about love and justice and mercy as being the point, but the Internet porn king who never repents will also end up in heaven. I'm sorry, what was the point of all that justice and mercy and goodness again? Oh, you had a better life? Not according to the Internet porn king who lives three doors down from you in heaven. Plus, this whole "you will have a better life as a Christian" argument is nothing but selfishness in religious garb. Everyone wants their best life now, even Nazis. Their best life now consisted of ethnic cleansing.

The point isn't to avoid hell; it's to love God.

Unfortunately, if you don't love God, He will send you to hell to keep heaven from becoming a bad neighborhood. That's the whole idea of having a relationship with God now. It prepares you for heaven. If you're not prepared, you don't go.

---

14. Albert Mohler, cited in Morgan and Peterson, *Hell Under Fire*, p. 37.

15. This joke is contractually required by anyone doing a rebuttal to one of Brian's books. In the industry we call this a "hack" joke.

Why Would God Send People to Hell?
Question Submitted by
the Sioux City Auxiliary Club

I think Tom Waits had it right in his song "Misery Is the River of the World" when he sang, "If there's one thing you can say about mankind—there's nothing kind about man." Surprisingly, this song was not a top 10 hit. It's a great song to sing in the shower if you don't want people yelling, "Hurry up in there." They will leave you alone when you're belting out that tune.

I concur, there's nothing kind about man.

Before I was a comedian, I worked as an operations supervisor for a major trucking company whose name I will not mention. Anyway, this excellent trucking company (I will even go so far as to say that they are "Arkansas Best Freight" line) had this terminal manager who was the boss from hell (kudos to Richard Lewis). This raises the question, If there is no hell, how then can one have a boss who originates from there?

Power corrupts? Business cards with the title "supervisor" corrupt.

My former boss was so verbally abusive that I would literally stand there unable to hold back the tears as he ranted about hiring such a moron. I wanted to ask, "If you hired a moron, what does that make you?" But I cried instead.

Forget about the problem of evil. What about the problem of buttheads?

That is why hell is a good idea—because of people. If it weren't for people, I probably wouldn't be pro-hell.

It's not that I don't love people. I just think they're horrible. I love people. I just hate their horribleness. People frighten me. But, for some reason, this happens every October 31.

Most people get offended when you tell them you think they're horrible, unless they're in customer service; then it's just the same old, same old. Our horribleness is the whole idea behind the right-to-privacy controversy. We don't want anyone to know what we're doing in private because it's horrible. Our grandmothers would die instantly if they knew. (May God rest her soul.)

No one thinks they deserve hell. That tells you something right there. We think we're great. That's why we don't like hell. We think it's unfair. Still, the one person that we all agree should be in hell is Hitler. Even people who hate the idea of hell will say, "If there is no hell in the afterlife, one should be invented just for Hitler. I hate to think of my ex-husband there all alone."

Brian tells us that theologian Lesslie Newbigin suggests that we shouldn't "speculate on the eternal destiny of others,"[16] unless, of course, you know them really well. Then it's easy to pick out which of your friends are probably going to hell. But according to Lesslie, you shouldn't do this. So, when the Bible says that you will know them by their fruit, you should ignore that. Just because you live like hell doesn't mean that you will go to hell. Well, unless you're living like hell when you die. Then I speculate that's where you will end up. I'm sure that Lesslie is a really smart man, but his position on hell is about as masculine as his name.

Now, I don't actually know if Lesslie is a beta male or not. He could be an alpha male with a beta male name. Obviously, making fun of someone's name is not a wise thing to do for a man named Thor. So, you can call me by my real name—Cheesewhiz.

Don't be misled thinking that only pagans, whores, strippers and comedians end up in hell. Hell will be full of respectable people, like schoolteachers and doctors and nurses and firemen. All it means when you're less obvious about your sins is that you're proud. That's the king of all sins. Congratulations—you've outsinned a porn king.

Way to excel!

---

16. McLaren, *The Last Word*, p. 103.

Without Hell,
Does Sin Matter Anymore?

Question Submitted by
the Redlands Cultural
Heritage Foundation

In Brian's gospel, he doesn't like to focus on sin, which is the same strategy that works for popular Broadway show tunes.[17] When people are worrying about their sins, they're only concerned with getting their butts into heaven. Then Cadillac sales drop. Thinking about sin just isn't good for the economy. "It makes you worry less about how bad humanity is and more about how mad the deity is."[18] What kind of gospel is that? The gospel is about making people holy, which means more justice and mercy and grace and care for others. To rid the world of societal evils such as hate, greed and reruns of *Friends*, first the individual must be rid of personal evil; and this is why God deals with us as individuals regarding personal salvation. It's not a salvation from hell, but from sin. Everyone wants to be saved from hell, but not everyone wants to be saved from his or her sins.

A gospel without sin is no gospel at all.

Write a snappy tune to that.

All I can say to losing sin as part of the gospel is, "Make sure you pack lots of evangelicalism, because it's going to get cold in Liberal City."

Part of our problem with hell is our problem with how we view our sins. We don't see our sins against God as being that egregious. Christopher Morgan writes, "The relationship and the offended party do matter. It is also important to remember that God is not only different from human beings in degree;

---

17. Name a Broadway show tune that focuses on sin. See?

18. McLaren, *The Last Word*, p. 135.

he is also different in being. If in a robbery, the gunman shoots and kills the owner of the house, he should receive a greater punishment than if he killed the family cat (as much as this writer loves cats!)"[19] However, if the robber were to shoot the dog, then the neighbors would finally be able to sleep soundly.

The old school view of hell is represented by a group of scholars who sometimes aren't so quick with irony, because they wrote a book called *Hell Under Fire*. (Gee, you think?) In this book they quote Thomas Oden, who wrote, "Hell expresses the intent of a holy God to destroy sin completely and forever. Hell is not merely a temporal no, but an eternal no to sin."[20]

If hell is not the last word for all who do evil, then it's not the ultimate rejection of it. (Sung to the tune of the "Jet Song" from *West Side Story*.)

What Is Hell Like?
Submitted by the Grand Rapids, Michigan, La Leche League

The big question people have about hell is—after someone dies, are they literally taken there in a hand basket?

Let me begin my explanation of what hell is like with an outdoor comedy event in Olympia, Washington. It was an outdoor event, which is perfect for the subject of hell. Outdoor events are not usually good for comedians. People are spread out all over the place. You can't hear the laughter. While I'm performing, a hearse with a bad muffler drives by, which I understand in a way. I mean, why fix your muffler for a dead guy? It's not like you're keeping him awake. I comment on it and everyone laughs. Suddenly, they're the best crowd I've

---

19. Morgan and Peterson, *Hell Under Fire*, p. 210.

20. Ibid., p. 17.

ever had . . . outdoors . . . as part of a car show.

After the comedy/car show was over, I was told that the church had arranged for a van to take me back to Seattle to a hotel near the airport. No big deal. I get in the van. The van begins to drive, but it doesn't head toward Seattle. It goes to a residence in Olympia and picks up a cranky old lady. I check with the driver to make sure he's taking us all to the airport and not making a detour to drop this lady off in hell. But he ignores me, attempting to find the next address on his massive list of people in Olympia without friends to take them to the airport. But he can't find the address. He says he's new to the job. Apparently, he's new to the city of Olympia, because he can't find crap. After 20 minutes, we're both helping him to find this place, which we finally do, but the joy is short-lived. He has another pick-up to make. Another address to not find. And another. And another. Until the van is full of angry people. Not one person in a 12-passenger van says a word.

What could we say?

"Do you hate the driver?"

"Yes. Yes, I do. But now I also secretly resent the church."

"That's nothing. I hate myself. I blame myself for taking this ride, because I took a shared-van ride once before and vowed I would never take another. But I forgot. Now, I hate myself for being an idiot."

"Down with shared-van rides!"

"Pull over, driver! We want to rock this vehicle onto its side!"

It's a van ride through hell, *The Great Divorce* come to life. *The Great Divorce* is a book by C. S. Lewis about a group of people who take a bus ride to hell. In this van, his plot doesn't seem far-fetched at all. I'm sure that God sends people to hell by the busload all the time. That's what makes it hell. You know where you're headed, but you never get there because the driver keeps stopping to pick someone else up.

I don't know why people are so hung up on God sending people to hell. What amazes me is that God likes us at all! Most of us can barely sit through a Thanksgiving dinner with some of our closest relatives. Why do you think God would want to hang out with us for all eternity?

That's why I think hell is a good idea—I've met some of you. Some of you were in the van. Look, there are days when I can barely stand myself. And if you're honest, you've had those days, too, when you can barely stand me.

Secretly, most people think hell is a good idea.

As a matter of fact, whenever someone has a good idea, it's always compared to hell. You tell someone your good idea and they will exclaim, "That's a hell of a good idea." An idea as good as hell—a helluva good idea. However, this is a phrase that will never be uttered after someone suggests you should take a shared-van ride to the airport.

The van driver drops everyone off at the airport terminal but me. I am the last passenger. He takes me to a one-star hotel the church has reserved for me and I tell him to keep going. (Now I know why Riders are so important.) The Hilton Garden Inn is just up the road, so I have him pull in there. I jump out, go to the back of the van to retrieve my luggage and one of my suitcases is missing. The driver accidentally gave one of my bags to another passenger. This seems totally reasonable at the time. I often hear people who don't travel much at the baggage claim saying, "I don't remember what my bag looks like." *Hey, enjoy my dirty underwear.*

If this doesn't seem frightening enough for hell, remember, this is only the ride to hell. Besides, we only spent three hours in the van. Imagine the driver saying, "Get back in," and off you go for 10,000 years. (Normally, if you drive yourself to hell, you can get there in half the time.)

Once the van stops, I can't give you grisly and ghastly descriptions of hell because we don't actually know what it's like. We only know it's as bad as burning alive or being alone in utter darkness forever.

That says enough.

Does the Punishment Fit the Crime?
Objections to Hell Submitted by the Dakota City Gardening Club

The most common moral objection to hell is the basic question, "Does the punishment fit the crime?" Why punish temporal sins for eternity? (I suppose only women know for sure.) In a book that covers four views of hell, I was astounded at how little space was given to this objection. Not only that, but my former boss wasn't mentioned by name even once. How is that possible in a book about hell?

Apparently all of us are bothered by different aspects of hell. I was never bothered by the concept, only by the duration. That's why I kept waiting for the debate about hell in this book to . . . well . . . heat up. Finally, on the second to the last page of the book, the Catholic guy gives the only answer to this objection. "The question of hell, then, is not: How can a God of love do such a thing to creatures? Rather, the question is: How seriously do we take our own God-given freedom?"[21]

Basically, God has given us that much freedom. You're free to date whoever you like and scorn her at your own discretion. If you want to go to hell, you can. The reason God gives us such freedom is that for love to truly matter, the object of devotion must be freely chosen. Jesus didn't chase down the rich young ruler when he walked away. He felt sad about the young man walking away, but He didn't chase after him. I don't know if this had anything to do with the fact that's it's hard to run in

---

21. Walvoord, Crockett, Hayes and Pinnock, *Four Views on Hell*, pp. 176-177.

sandals, but the young ruler was free to walk away, and Jesus gave him that freedom.

McLaren says that even if people are damned by their own freedom of choice, then freedom of choice might not be that great a gift because it's basically like giving a six-year-old a loaded gun.[22] Well, if someone teaches the six-year-old kid how to handle the gun, he might not kill anyone. That is, if you give him all the candy and ice cream he wants. However, comparing an adult's freedom of choice to giving a six-year-old a gun is like comparing apples to Uzis.

Anti-Christian comedian Bill Hicks once said, "Christianity is such an odd religion. The whole image is eternal suffering awaits anyone who questions God's infinite love. *Believe or die.* Thank you for giving, Lord . . . for all those options."

David Wilkerson of the Broadway Tabernacle in New York City once said, "People will curse God because He made it too easy, too simple. When people see the simplicity of the gospel, that will be their torment."

Even with the simplicity of the gift of salvation, people still refuse to choose Life.

Now that's odd.

Who Gets Saved from Hell?
Question Submitted by the Emergent Village People

People have always hated the concept of hell; but in the same sense, people have also hated the concept of grace being preached without compromise.[23] People have a problem with certain sinners getting into heaven, because of the Christian concept of salvation by grace alone. They hate the idea of good

---

22. McLaren, *The Last Word*, p. 102.

23. Gregory A. Boyd, *Repenting of Religion: Turning from Judgment to the Love of God* (Grand Rapids, MI: Baker Books, 2004), p. 42.

people going to hell and bad people going to heaven, like a convicted rapist or serial killer who gets jailhouse religion. From an evangelical perspective, many people encounter Christ in prison. There will probably be all kinds of rapists and murderers in heaven. (Would you like to join our church?) It's a caricature of grace, of course, but the point remains valid—you're only saved by grace through faith in Christ and not by any of your good deeds.

The theological view of conversion is that when a murderer or rapist or even a racist encounters Christ, they are changed internally, from the very core of their being. They are no longer the same person. Now they know how to vote. And this is why presidential candidates visit Bob Jones University.

This brings me to another reason why hell is a good idea—because of some people who call themselves Christians. The problem with Christianity has never been with Jesus; it's with some of us who claim to be His followers.

I'd love to see a Klan member at the Judgment Seat of Christ. Jesus says to him, "Depart from me. I never knew you."

The Klan member is surprised. He's been a church member all his life. He believes the Bible. He's been baptized, dunked under water no less. He will ask incredulously, "You never knew me?"

And Jesus will answer, "Hey, man, you had a sheet over your head. How was I supposed to recognize you?"

The Klan makes hell a good idea.

Now, in no way am I implying that the Klan and Bob Jones University are in cahoots. All I'm saying is that some alumni of Bob Jones University may have been Klan members.

The End of Hell

As I'm finishing up this chapter, I must confess that it doesn't feel good to write about such negative subjects as this. This is why I'd like to at least end on an encouraging note: I'd like to encourage you to not go to hell.

There.

I feel better now, and isn't that the point of life?

After my plane lands, I walk to my car and once again I am reminded of the reasonableness of hell. My car has a new dent—a very real and noticeable dent. And this is why I think hell is a good idea. Come on, humans. We're despicable. We lie whenever it benefits us, like say for instance, when you back into my parked car at the airport and leave me with a dent that I have to pay for out-of-pocket because of my deductible. You should have left a note. You should have taken responsibility for your actions. You hit. You ran. It cost me money.

"Will not the Judge of all the earth do right?" (Gen. 18:25).

Hell is a good idea.

Driving home, feeling very self-righteous about how people don't own up to their actions, I hit a bump, my glove box pops open and five unpaid speeding tickets spill out.

Hell is a very good idea.

CHAPTER 10

A New Kind of Hell

(Brimstone and Punchlines)

When I was in second grade, Carla Sublet was in my class, and her mom was also our teacher, so telling her to go to hell during recess, in retrospect, was not a politically astute move. Secretly, I had a crush on Carla Sublet every year of elementary school, but thanks to reruns of *Leave It to Beaver*, I learned that boys weren't supposed to like girls until they were older.[1] So, I emulated the Beave by alternately treating her nice and then telling her to go to hell, a pattern of treating women that would last for years to come.

This chapter is about Jesus' view of hell, a place to which He sometimes told people they were going, but in a much wiser way so as to avoid staying in for recess for a month.

In today's age of peace, love and misunderstanding, hell is something that makes church leaders sweat even when they're not trying to be ironic. Many pastors now question whether Jesus spoke of hell in the way Christians have traditionally interpreted it—as a real place of eternal suffering and torment. This doctrine has been a fundamental Bible teaching and has always been effective in tandem with yelling "Stop that!" as in "Stop that or you'll go to hell." The new doctrine of hell, as

---

1. However, the subject of this chapter is not the anti-feminist aspects of *Leave It to Beaver*, though I would certainly argue that the sitcom is no friend to second-grade girls, or women in general.

you'll see, is not nearly as effective: "Stop that or . . . nothing of serious consequence will happen to you."

The fact that Jesus talked so much about hell may also explain why people sometimes waited to beat Him up after He preached. Only once in my comedy career have I worried about somebody waiting to beat me up after a show, that is, someone who wasn't related to me. I remember the heckler very well, the color of his shirt, what his knuckles were wearing. I was onstage somewhere in North Dakota, most likely Grand Forks, where they had a regular gig for years in a hotel that was a wagon train come to life, barroom brawls and all; wagon wheel lamps hung from the ceiling and a comedian performed for the blank stares of 4-H Club champions. Having just played Seattle, I purchased some funky-looking shoes that had a back strap. Men's strappy shoes. In North Dakota. Do you sense a storm a brewin'?

Comedians follow a rule of thumb before they put down a heckler. Never do it unless you've really been provoked, or the entire crowd has witnessed it and you think you can outrun the guy.

This guy in the front row leaned into his girlfriend or sister or parole officer—maybe she was all three—and made a derogatory and uninformed remark about my sexuality. Then he said, "Those are gay shoes." First, I had him repeat the line aloud so that everyone could hear, something I learned from my second-grade teacher, Mrs. Sublet. Then I looked down at my shoes, back at the guy and said, "I could've sworn I bought the straight shoes. I thought these loafers felt a little light."

It's always amazing how naive hecklers are for even trying. All they have is a voice in the darkness. I have a sound system. It's never a fair fight. Plus, I'm sober. Alcohol and comedy— does that make any sense? "Let's go to a comedy club and drink a depressant. That way they'll balance each other out and we'll leave in the same state as when we entered."

Actually, I don't even remember what I said to this guy. Something along the lines of, "I'm sorry, but I don't know how to deal with you. I'm a comic, not a proctologist."

What on earth was I thinking? I couldn't run in those shoes. They had straps. And I violated rule number 3 of the comedian's general rule of thumb with hecklers. I'm lucky the comedians' union didn't fine me.

He pulled his ball cap down a little tighter and yelled back at me, "After the show, I'm gonna kick you're butt straight to hell!" Except he said it more like a trucker. Or a sailor. North Dakota. Okay, trucker.

Then I had to wait out the rest of the show to see if he was going to kick my butt straight to hell. I wasn't sure if he would follow through with his threat due to the fact that he was a human being, not the most reliable of species. By the looks of him, though, I was pretty sure he knew how to get to hell.

People are continually brandishing the phrase "go to hell," totally unaware of what Christ said about the subject. So, after reading this chapter, I'm hoping that my mother-in-law will at least be able to say this to me with a better understanding.

To research the subject of hell, I took a yellowish-red colored pencil (appropriate for the subject matter, I figured) and marked every passage in the New Testament where Jesus spoke of hell. ("So, real theologians ain't got nothin' on me," spoken like Denzel Washington in *Training Day*.)

The first time Jesus mentions hell is in Matthew 5:21-22: "You have heard that it was said to the people long ago, 'Do not murder, and anyone who murders will be subject to judgment.' But I tell you that anyone who is angry with his brother will be subject to judgment. Again, anyone who says to his brother, 'Raca,' is answerable to the Sanhedrin. But anyone who says, 'You fool!' will be in danger of the fire of hell."

The first thing I noticed about this passage in my Bible is that Jesus speaks in red, which obviously implies a strong belief in hell. As a matter of fact, whenever Jesus speaks on any subject in the New Testament, He speaks in red, implying, "Listen to what I have to say or you could end up in hell." So, the implication of hell is always there when Jesus speaks.

And who are the Sanhedrin? I think they're Jewish tribal judges who named themselves after a maximum strength sinus medication.

The second thing I noticed about this passage is that I know what "you fool" means and that is what troubles me. I basically make my living by pointing out foolishness and the fools behind it. Sometimes the fool is me, but still. It's not so comforting.

Some Bible teachers think this passage might be suggesting that a really bad attitude can send you to hell. This is not good news for teenagers or comedians. Jesus wasn't saying this to the religious leaders of His day, either. He was talking to average mountainside picnickers,[2] according to the text. So, Jesus is basically saying, "People think that murder's about the worst thing you can do, right? Well, anger's right up there with murder. *Murder is just anger communicated really well.* And expressing your anger by calling people nasty and indefinable words means that your eternal destiny could be whatever I mean by hell."

What *did* Jesus mean by hell when He spoke of it, because in His lifetime, I'm pretty sure He'd never been to Oakland. (Honorable mention for hell goes to the Oakland International Airport.)

Rob Bell, master of all things ancient and Jewish, writes, "The word hell in English is the word gehenna in Greek. Gehenna is a reference to the Valley of Hinnom, a ravine on the

2. Picnickers who incidentally forgot to bring food to the picnic.

south side of the city of Jerusalem. Garbage, trash, wild animals fighting over scraps of food, a fire burning—a place of waste and destruction."[3]

It was basically like going to a Raider's game. (Okay, maybe Jesus had been to Oakland.)

When Jesus spoke of hell, people had a word picture in their minds. They could picture hell and its destruction, but they also understood that Jesus was speaking metaphorically. He didn't mean this particular dump was hell, only that hell was like this dump. It would be like saying, "Anyone who says, 'You fool!' will be in danger of an apartment in Biloxi." He doesn't mean that hell is an apartment in Biloxi, only that hell is as bad as an apartment in Biloxi.[4]

To bring dramatic tension to this subject, if hell isn't dramatic enough for you, I will contrast my view of what Jesus meant by hell with Brian McLaren's new kind of hell. In his book *The Last Word and the Word After That*, he claims that Jesus didn't invent hell. It wasn't His idea.

If that is the case, then I would also like to add that having sex with only one woman for the rest of your life was not Jesus' idea either. Now, all I need are some ancient sources to reinforce this view and a less intelligent wife.

Brian bases his view that Jesus didn't invent hell on the fact that other ancient writers told stories of magical trees, like the one in the Garden of Eden, and of snakes as demons. But maybe these ancient people actually did encounter snakes as demons.[5] I don't think demons taking the form of animals is so far-

---

3. *Velvet Elvis: Repainting the Christian Faith* (Grand Rapids, MI: Zondervan, 2006), p. 57.

4. Third runner-up for something analogous to hell is Mississippi.

5. If you think that's farfetched, then read *Spirit of the Rainforest*, a modern-day account of a shaman chief in the Amazon rain forests. It's an amazing story of how shamans from various tribes would communicate with spirits. The shamans said the spirits often took the form of animals. It's a fascinating read.

fetched. My entertainment lawyer is a snake who has taken the form of a human. It happens all the time.

Brian says that Jesus took the idea of hell and used it against the Pharisees who were using the idea of hell to scare people into "flying right." So, Jesus used hell to get the Pharisees to fly right. Apparently, the important thing to Jesus is to fly right, and this is why I'm sure He's so pleased with the *Left Behind* series. It's all about flying Christians.

If hell is only a warning but is not an actual spiritual state, then it's really a hollow warning, much like "you better not pout, you better not cry." I can pout and cry all I want now that I know Santa punched out at nine and walked home from the mall holding his beard in one hand and a six-pack of Bud Light in the other. Of course, I can't imagine that Jesus is just trying to scare us with something that doesn't really exist. Jesus is not like the Bush administration, and hell is not like weapons of mass destruction.

The problem, in my expert comedic analysis, is that we have interpreted the warnings of Jesus about hell as pertaining to the next life when, in fact, they are warnings about this life. Our emphasis has been wrong. Jesus didn't come to save people from hell.

"Well, what's the point of the gospel then?" asks Morph.

Man, have we really strayed that far from the point of it all? I'm sorry, but it's something I must now address because my imaginary character, Morph, brought it up. I can't just ignore his question. I'd like to convey a Christian attitude even to the imaginary.

When people think that getting saved from hell is what Jesus came to do for them, they misunderstand His mission. Jesus came to save His people "from their sins" (Matt. 1:21). This, in turn, will save them from hell because it saves them from greed, lust, envy, lust, bitterness, anger, lust, posters of Jessica

Simpson,[6] lust and other conditions of the heart that lead to hell on Earth, such as lust. If you don't get saved from anything in this life, then you don't get saved from anything in the next life. This doesn't mean that meritorious works save you. It just means that true faith affects change in a person's character, which in turn affects his or her choice of poster art—I suggest something with kittens and cute sayings. (Dogs playing poker is always humorous, but the poker is theologically problematic because whenever you tell dogs to "double down," they just turn their heads and stare at you. Dogs are incredibly dumb.)

If you're not making society better by showing compassion, extending mercy, standing for justice, living with complete integrity and avoiding posters of Jessica Simpson, then you're making society worse. That's hell on Earth. And when your heart wraps around greed, lust, envy, lust, bitterness, lies, lust, anger, hatred, lust and all the rest, including lust, your heart would actually be more at home in hell. All that God's doing by sending you there is accommodating your needs.

Some people are ready for hell. They live with the values of the devil, which will sound corny because no one believes in the devil anymore either. Which is also odd, because without the devil how do you explain the career of Justin Timberlake? (As a comedian, I am required to give equal time to male pop stars as well.)

My good friend, comedian and actor—now I have to pay a union fee or something for telling you he's an actor—Bone Hampton once said, "When the devil shows up, he looks just like us." Then I asked Bone, "Who are you really?"

Jesus doesn't send people to hell because of the things they do. Jesus isn't about rules; He's all about the heart, the core of

---

6. It's really quite sad that we need to be saved from the likes of Jessica Simpson, because her dad used to be a youth pastor before he became a high-powered manager who brags about his daughter's, er—assets.

your being and what burps up out of it. It's the heart that He's concerned with—who you are deep, deep down beneath your gooey insides. That's why He sends people to hell based on the condition of their heart, like those people who act all nicey-nice outwardly but still have a rotten heart. People need new hearts, hearts that are more conducive to posters of kittens hanging from chin-up bars.

The fact remains, some people are going to hell and some people are going to heaven. There's this push within evangelicalism to eliminate the "us" and "them" mentality, the "in" and "out" categorizing of people. But some people are not "in" good standing with God. They are "outside" of His desires for them. We don't know who exactly. Unfortunately, even after chest X-rays, it's hard to determine if Jesus is in someone's heart.

But we all start there, as God's enemies. No one's in because they're better. We're in because the invitation is open to everyone. It's all-inclusive. You've been invited to the party, but that doesn't mean you have to attend. The problem with eliminating the in/out language of salvation is that it's in the Bible. Jesus said in Matthew 13:49-50, "This is how it will be at the end of the age. The angels will come and separate the wicked from the righteous and throw them into the fiery furnace, where there will be weeping and gnashing of teeth."

So there you have it. The angels are much more reliable than Santa Claus, because, apparently, they have the list and don't even have to check it twice. And whatever hell is, according to this text, there is going to be weeping and gnashing of teeth, much like listening to a Justin Timberlake CD.

Jesus told a story about the rich man and Lazarus and treated it like it was an incident in the afterlife. Jesus said that when the rich man died, he found himself in hell, "where he was in torment" (Luke 16:23). Apparently, there is a mall in hell where you spend eternity waiting for someone to pick out a handbag.

Now, I think torment basically means, ah . . . torment. And to make the verse mean something else, I think you really have to twist things. It only has a few options as to its meaning. You see? This was written 2,000 years ago (give or take), in another language, and we still kind of get it.

Words still have meaning.

Yippie!

David Wilkerson, from *The Cross and the Switchblade* fame, and founding pastor of Times Square Church in New York City, said in a sermon on hell, "When you get to heaven, you don't get everything all at once. It's not static. You don't suddenly get the full revelation of Jesus. You'll be learning all throughout eternity. The joy will be ever greater, the ecstasy, everything. In hell there is an ever-increasing knowledge of what was missed. An ever-increasing torment. An ever-increasing sense of being cast farther and farther away from the presence of God for eternity."

Now that would be a sobering statement even if it came from the mouth of Pat Boone wearing a milk mustache—who played David Wilkerson in the movie version of *The Cross and the Switchblade*, where the rumble scenes were less realistic than the dancing fighters in *West Side Story*.

Here's something pleasing to those of you who find hell an uncomfortable topic or even more so mixed with comedy. The Gospel of John doesn't mention hell once.[7]

No hellfire and brimstone, *or punchlines*.

Now, I would say you can argue biblically that you don't need to emphasize hell when presenting the gospel because that's what the Gospel of John is—a gospel presentation. He certainly didn't emphasize hell. He didn't even use the word once, though Jesus still speaks in red in his gospel, too, so the subtext of hell is always there.

---

7. It only has a few sentences of implication where Jesus says, "Those who have done good will rise to live, and those who have done evil will rise to be condemned" and "whoever believes in him shall not perish" and "whoever believes in him is not condemned."

Still, I don't think the conventional view of hell is "widely known and defended" as Brian McLaren contends. It's the Christian's dirty little secret. I agree with Church historian Martin Marty: "Hell has disappeared and no one noticed." No one noticed because no one was talking about it. Hell has been lost, which is ironic in light of the traditional view that lost people go there. The most pressing question now is, If we lose hell, where are we going to put everyone?

There's another irony about the contemporary disregard for hell. Many current Christian leaders, besides Brian, are upset by the idea of God sending people to hell, but no one's complaining about God sending fallen angels to hell. How come God hasn't worked out a plan of salvation for demons? Why no compassion for demons, my friends? The silly Universalists (yes, you're all silly, Sweethearts of Sigma Chi) never talk about the ultimate salvation of demons. Why so cold-hearted?

I find it fascinating that people want to be safe from the idea of hell. The idea scares them, probably because all ideas imply possibilities. We will never be free from the possibility of hell as long as the idea persists. You have to destroy the idea if you want to be free.

To hell with hell.

This is my generation's chant.

I protest.

Hell is a good idea.

I think hell makes the gospel even better. When is good news the best? When you've got some really bad news before it. For example, try this line out on whoever you're dating: "I don't think we should see each other anymore. (Two, three, four.) Will you marry me?"

You see how that works? Bad news followed by good news. It predates the good news/bad news scenario that has been a comedy staple for years. Good news: You get an expensive designer bag. Bad news: It's a colostomy bag.

Please tip your wait staff.

Another idea about hell is that it's really just representative of a wasted life. As if it's not a real place of torment but just represents the regret we will feel if we fail to live up to our potential. Brian asks us, "Wouldn't that make you weep and gnash your teeth?"

No. Not really. People enjoy wasting their lives. To many people, myself among them for many years, watching TV all day while stoned is living life to the fullest. That's why they're doing it. They want the abundant life, man.

Presently, I could live with constant regret because I already know that if "God has a plan for your life," I missed it. I have wasted my youth. Even now, I'm a comedian for God's sake (literally), but I still wonder if I shouldn't write serious and pretty thoughts like Donald Miller, someone who would never make fun of Jessica Simpson. I'd like to write like Donald Miller, but he's really smart and a really excellent writer. Sure, I can write, but he's a *writer*. There's a difference.

Let me demonstrate.

Here is a paragraph from Don Miller's book *Through Painted Deserts*:

> *We move with new and appreciated quickness toward a sinking sun that sets to flame the backs of close and distant hills, causing clouds to flare in violent strips and tall trees to lay their shadows across the road like nightclothes across a bed. Oklahoma has no better show than evening.* [p. 37]

My version would be:

> *We drive fast toward Oklahoma because we want to get there SOONER than later.* (Get it? *Sooner?* Yeehaw!)

You see?

There's a difference.

My point being, I could be wasting my life right now, which means I could be wasting your life right now.

Sorry about that.

Here's what's terrifying about dying: Facing what you've become after your life is over and the consequences of what your heart reveals about your true love. "Imagine what it means for people to stand before God in the presence of truth," McLaren writes, "Nothing could be more serious than that."[8] Sure it could. There could also be a really massive crowd. And loud speakers. Kind of like a music festival where everyone's sins get outed. Actually, the most serious thing won't be standing before God; it will be God explaining the consequences of our lives to us while we stand before Him. People fear the Truth because of the consequences of not following the Truth. And this is why we also fear Death.

During my last trip to Fresno, I happened to run into Death in the parking lot of what was once a thriving shopping plaza that had recently been converted into a church facility. Taking advantage of the opportunity, I asked Death to Starbucks, where I proceeded to interview him. The transcript from the interview (which I recorded with a program on my laptop called Sound Studio) is below.

Thor: What's the biggest misconception people have about you?

Death: Well, that it's my fault. I just do what I'm told. I'm given a list and I do my job. Look, I'm living a purpose-driven life, too. It's just that my purpose in God's plan is to make sure you die on time.

---

8. Brian McLaren, *The Last Word and the Word After That: A Tale of Faith, Doubt and a New Kind of Christianity* (San Francisco: Jossey-Bass, 2005), p. 80.

Thor: Do you ever feel bad about what you do?

Death: Could you hand me a Sweet'N Low?

Thor: Sure.

Death: Do you feel bad about being a comedian?

Thor: I don't see how that's relevant.

Death: Well, if you haven't noticed, I'm at a lot of your shows.

Thor: What?

Death: That silence where you could hear a pin drop—

Thor: That's you?

Death: That's me. Honestly, though, it's one of my better gigs. No one . . . you know. I'm just there to make sure some of those jokes are never told again.

Thor: I'm sure my audience appreciates it.

Death: It's what I do.

Thor: So, you're not just involved in the taking of lives?

Death: No, no, no. Remember George Michael? The singer. He's not really popular anymore, is he? You have me to thank for that. His career is dead.

Thor: Wake me up before you go-go.

Death: Personally, that's why I think that using current pop references in your comedy is a bad idea. Because they are soon dated.

Thor: If you don't think I should use the Jessica Simpson and Justin Timberlake references, just come out and say it. I mean, you're Death. Don't be coy.

Death: It's just my opinion.

Thor: Anyway, what other aspects of your work are we unfamiliar with?

Death: Well, sometimes I'll just sit in the living room of some suburban home and watch TV. I don't touch anybody. I just sit and watch *Lost* and *24*. And you won't believe what happens. Pretty soon this couple isn't touching anymore. They snap at each other continually.

Thor: You kill marriages?

Death: Thank you. Someone finally said it.

Thor: You are much more diverse than . . . than I thought you would be.

Death: Oh, people misjudge me all the time. I've got to be going. I'm due at an accident on Moreno Beach Drive.

Thor: That sickle. Do you really use that for anything?

Death: People in jungles, they gotta die, don't they?

Thor: You take them out with a sickle?

Death: No, dummy, the curved blade is great for cutting tall grass.

Thor: Tall grass?

Death: They're hard to get to.

Thor: Right. Hey, one last question.

Death: Make it quick. That's how I work.

Thor: What can you tell us about hell? What's it like?

Death: That's not my area. I'm the wages of sin. I just deliver the packages. Kind of like a spiritual UPS.

Thor: Is there actual fire or brimstone? Have you seen anything?

(No response.)

Thor: Hello?

(Dead silence.)

Fire and brimstone and darkness and weeping and chewing your lips in agony are not the point of the images of hell. The point is that it expresses God's view of sin. That's how much God hates our war, and the exploitation and oppression of people, and child pornography and neat suburban divorces. God hates sin so much that He created a dumping ground for it.

That's old-fashioned Bible-thumping scary. That's what we fear the most, though. Being seen as Bible-thumpers. So, we raise our voices: "Hell is unfair of God. It's unjust of God."

I think just the opposite—hell magnifies human injustice. It shows us how much God hates sin, because by it we destroy each other.

Whether you believe in hell or not, one thing is certain . . . Death is soon and coming.

Have a nice day.

CHAPTER 11

So Full of Grace, We're Full of . . .

(Divorce and Outreach Poker Night, an Overview)

Making fun of evangelicals isn't something that makes me feel guilty, because a joke is often just a rebuke with a punch line. Rarely do I question myself when satirizing my tribe, primarily because we should feel ashamed of some things. For instance, I received a flyer in the mail advertising a Christian health insurance company.

Christian health insurance?

Do they reimburse for healings?

Will they cover my preexisting conditions? How about the predestined ones? Are those the same thing?

Do they cover wrongful crucifixion?

How do you handle Christian insurance theologically?

"My friend has a plank in his eye; I have a log in mine. Am I liable?"

I consider my ridicule of things like Christian health insurance—or Christian breath mints, or Christian movies about the apocalypse with no special effects, or Christian Universalists—consistent with God's grace, because sometimes grace exposes us. This idea of Christian health insurance deserves some exposure, if you will. It's about as helpful as the long-standing evangelical idea of "fire insurance," meaning that some people convert just because they want to avoid hell. Mostly, we blame the hellfire and brimstone folks for this tactic, which probably doesn't happen much anymore. Ironically, all the hellfire and brimstone preachers have died and gone to heaven. Contemporary evangelism lures people into becoming Christians with the promise of eternal life. It's the inverse of the hellfire preaching, though just as manipulative and resulting in just as many lame-duck believers, some who will go on to offer us Christian health insurance and a phenomenon known as Christian comedy.

Many Christians are confused about what really constitutes saving faith; and this is why sometimes in the offering plate under a pile of singles you find a matchbook from *Skanky Babes Gentlemen's Club*.

The apparent confusion comes to life through the problem of divorce in the Church, or should I say, executives come to life whenever a new secretarial temp shows up at work. That problem and others depict our theological weaknesses when we say we're "saved by grace through faith" but live lives that aren't saved from anything.

In conjunction with saving faith, of course, is the Christian concept of grace, immortalized in songs like "Just as I Am" and "If You're Saved, Why Do You Still Smell Like Schnapps?"

Personally, I think the world's view of Christ and the Church might be better off if some people who claim to be Christians had a less secure view of their salvation. You know what would really cut down on hypocrisy in the Church? If more Christians got saved. Forgive me for saying this, albeit only if you're filled with grace, but sometimes I think we're so full of grace that we're full of crap. (I'd like to use another word, but some of you don't have *that* much grace.) What I mean is that Antinomianism is alive and well in the twenty-first-century Church, that is to say, a view of grace that divorces faith from behavior.

It's what Dietrich Bonhoeffer called "cheap grace." Apparently, his book *The Cost of Discipleship* wasn't a bestseller because his corrective never caught on.

Expand my territory—bestseller.

Die to self—not so much.

Sometimes I wonder if I'm really saved, if I'm really going to heaven, if I'm not just self-deceived and if smoking really isn't the best idea. The same kind of thoughts many of us have while pumping gas. I know that assurance of salvation is a big deal for evangelicals. If you're not sure you're going to heaven when you die, you can't answer the most trite question in all of Christendom: "If you were to die today, do you know where you would spend eternity?"

"No, but can you turn on pump number three?"

"Put out your cigarette, please."

"Man, you got no grace."

When did insecurity get such a bad rap? When I'm a little insecure about losing my job, I improve my performance. (Happy anniversary, honey!) So, what you're telling me is that Christians can't be fired? No wonder we currently have such a bad reputation. We have the most powerful union boss in the whole universe.

What's wrong with a little temporary insecurity to balance our eternal security? An old evangelist once said that a true Christian would serve Jesus whether she is going to heaven or not. Now that's customer service.

Church folks get snippy when you imply that some of us who claim to be Christians might not actually be Christians. I mean, we think we're Christians, but our thoughts and actions testify against us, as do some of the Internet sites we visit.

Leonard Ravenhill, a fire-breathing evangelist and author, speculates that only 7 percent of those who claim to be Christians are really Christians. He bases this statistic on the fact that approximately 93 percent of us Christians really suck at it.

Still, people get upset when you mention it.

Several weeks ago, I was speaking at a Celebrate Recovery evening. If you're not familiar with Celebrate Recovery groups, well let me just say they have lived life hard-pressed, dragged and screaming, hung out to dry—all that and more. They're much more festive than those Celebrate Teatotaling groups. You could open your set for a Celebrate Recovery group by saying, "If Jesus has been good to you say, '$#%@, yeah! Jesus has been good to me!'" and you wouldn't offend a hair on their recovering heads.

On the other hand, if you mention the divorce stats of evangelicals, you might offend the singer you're working with.

I do this bit called "Divorce and Bible Sex" about, well, divorce and sex. It's mildly controversial because some Christian groups don't even like the word "sex" mentioned, let alone substituting $#!% for certain words. However, sex is a gift from God, and we should not be ashamed of it. Granted, celibacy is also a gift from God. But let's be honest, it's kind of like getting socks for Christmas. Anyway, during my set at the recovery meeting, I said, "The fact that the divorce rate among evangelical Christians is higher than the general population's certainly doesn't do anything to glorify the power of God to change lives."

Then on to comedy.

After I finished my little comedy bit, the singer said to the audience, "I heard the remarks about our divorce rate. Well, that is just classic performance-based religion." Then he went on a classic spiel extolling cheap grace. Another platform speaker so full of grace that he's full of . . . it.

Look, before you drown me like Calvin would, I know that we're saved by grace alone through faith and not by anything we do (thus my freedom to type the symbols $#%@, which represent a bad word); but we have this cockeyed way of living it out and presenting it to the world at large.

Grace is demonstrated in personal relationships, and most clearly in marriage relationships. God used an entire chapter of the Bible to analogize His grace toward us in the Song of Solomon. "Marriage" itself is an interesting word study. You might notice that the first syllable of the word "Marriage" is "Mar," as in blight, spoil, tarnish, ruin . . . I could go on. In fact there are three words in "Marriage"—Marr, I and Age. Translation; I'm old and ruined.

We need grace.

Still, if your view of grace allows you to leave your wife, move in with a younger woman, live with her until you go through with a divorce, then not marry her because, well, you are still not sure if what you're doing is the right thing, all the while oblivious to the ramifications of what this is doing to your now 8-year-old daughter and 6-year-old son, then your view of grace is . . . cockeyed, pal.

(Deep breath.)

Based on a true story, by the way.

Now, hold on there Philip Yancey, I'm not saying there is no room for grace in divorce among Christians. I don't know the circumstances behind the singer's divorce. (As it turns out, he was divorced.) Yes, we forgive and forget (though our lawyers are kind enough to remind us). This whole divorce business in the Church gets very messy, partly due to the fact that men are not good at making beds. I'm not a blanket[1] legalist in this matter, but Jesus was pretty clear. I know. Because six months after I married, I went looking for loopholes. Fourteen years later, my wife and I are happily married. But what other choice do we have, really? If you know you're not going anywhere, you make things work. I'm so committed to my wife that I won't even Google "a woman." I won't even cheat on her in my dreams. And

---

1. No pun intended.

believe you me, I have plenty of opportunity to cheat on her. In my dreams. I probably turn down Penelope Cruz once a week. I think. It's hard to tell because she's speaking Spanish. Instead of begging me to run off with her, she could just be telling me to get off her lawn. And then I'm chased by giant mushrooms. I don't know why. It's a dream.

Jesus said regarding divorce, "I tell you that anyone who divorces his wife, except for marital unfaithfulness, and marries another woman commits adultery" (Matt. 19:9).

The disciples basically felt the same way we do. "Hey, the eunuchs got it easy."[2]

Then some zealot stepped forward with a knife: "That can be arranged."[3]

Then Jesus said something really interesting: "Not everyone can accept this word, but only those to whom it has been given" (Matt. 19:11).

Is this a trick?

Okay, you've just read this word. In other words, this word has been given to you. Tag. You're it. No divorce. Pass it on.

Or does Jesus mean that staying married is a special gift, like celibacy? There's a new out for you: "Staying married wasn't my gift." I think that's a stretch. What I call theological aerobics.

If you're married to someone you don't love, look on the bright side: When they get upset—it's not that big of a deal.

Our society has lost the concept of marriage as an institution that is larger than any two individuals, primarily because the Church has lost this view. The stability of our marriages is important to society as a whole, providing structure, support, growth and children who won't kill people. According to a study

---

2. What they actually said was, "If this is the situation between a husband and wife, it is better not to marry" (Matt. 19:10).

3. This is implied in the text by comedians.

by the Department of Health and Human Services, "healthy marriages evidence fewer pathologies, such as crime, welfare dependency and kicking the guy dressed as Captain Hook in the shins at Disneyland." Okay, they didn't mention the part about kicking Captain Hook in the shins, but you can be sure that's displaced anger directed at a spouse.

Jesus said, "the two become one flesh" (Matt. 19:5). You and your spouse are one person. That means that as a couple, you are twice as annoying as when you're alone. When a marriage falls apart, it's not just between a husband and a wife, and their children who grow up to become gang members. It affects other marriages. The strength of one marriage will encourage weaker marriages, and the fall of a strong marriage will discourage weaker marriages, resulting in a decline of Tupperware parties. But, unfortunately, nothing in our society is bigger than the individual. That's really all postmodernism is: hyper-hyper-individualism.[4] We change our minds every five minutes based on individual preferences.

"I'll follow Jesus until one of His followers makes me mad."

"Hey, it was nice having you."

We say we want community, meaning that we want a bunch of people we can hang with; but we don't want to be responsible for influencing their lives. And we certainly don't want them speaking into our lives. "My friend, I think you might have a substance abuse problem."

"Really? Well, if the substance is *you* and it's about to be abused by me, then, yeah, I think you're right."

Cheap grace only exacerbates these situations. After divorce, people move on as best they can after someone has left their life in ruins. Cheap grace will not help clean up all the rubble.

---

4. I heard one of Ken Meyer's guests on the *Mars Hill Audio Journal* say this. You'll have to ask Ken who it was.

Those who've been hurt must do that bit by dusty bit with the grace of God, a costly grace. Cheap grace might get us into these situations, but it's another kind of grace that gets us out.

(Look, I don't plan on being a popular keynote speaker.)

Still, I think there's something wrong with our view of grace if telling Christians to stay married is seen as classic works-based religion.

"Don't have sex outside of marriage."

"Wow! He's harsh."

"And don't murder your spouse."

"Man, he's so legalistic."

Ladies and gentlemen, might I remind you that Hosea the prophet married a prostitute for the sake of a sermon illustration.[5] You think maybe we Christians might stay married to illustrate the grace of God? *You're* a bonehead and God loves *you*. Go and do likewise to your spouse.

On a side note, if you're a Christian and your spouse has cheated on you, then you're good to go. Really. I have nothing but grace for you. Let the door hit him/her on the way out. Unless you want to use your spouse as a sermon illustration.

Don't misunderstand me, because I really, truly, absolutely, undeniably understand the circumstances that vary from one marriage to another. Adultery is just the clearest out.[6] So, if you're

---

5. Okay there, junior Bible scholars, I know that Hosea's example had to do with a nation's unfaithfulness to God, not with marriage in particular. My point is using life as an illustration the way Hosea did.

6. I'll give you some more loopholes besides adultery, so get ready to speed dial your lawyer: (1) Child molestation. If your spouse molests one of your children, that's a type of rape. Get out, press charges and lock him up. (Oh, I'm taking a shot here and guessing it might be a guy doing the molesting.) (2) Because men can be hard to reach and often need to be forcibly humbled, separation is in order for any of the following circumstances: physical or verbal abuse of a spouse or child, extreme pornography. (3) If someone purposely misrepresents himself or herself before you marry him or her. Let's say you marry someone and after you're married your spouse mentions, "By the way, I'm not really rich, or a Christian." Get the annulment, baby.

unhappily married, you might want to stack your home Bible study group with attractive people and encourage your spouse to mingle.

I'm primarily focusing on marriage and divorce here because it's indicative of a severe theological problem within the Church, namely, our view of grace.

Hey, Preacher People, if your views on grace expressed from the pulpit have allowed some dense guy to leave his family and then later remark that he wants a divorce now so that he "can start going to church again," then you have not rightly explained grace.

(Based on a true story.)

I know a Christian lady who left her husband because she wasn't happy in the marriage. That's it. He didn't cheat on her. He didn't beat on her. He just wasn't a great communicator. She felt emotionally unfulfilled. So, she left and married another Christian man who talked more and also sang. Now they sing in church together.

(Based on a true story.)

If your view of grace allows for these scenarios, then let me say with as much grace as I can—you're full of $#%@.

Philip Yancey shares a story in his book *What's So Amazing About Grace?* about a divorced friend who was standing in church with her 15-year-old daughter when the pastor's wife approached her and said, "I hear you're divorcing. What I can't understand is that if you love Jesus and he loves Jesus, why are you doing that?"

Philip explains the situation: "The pastor's wife had never really spoken to my friend before, and her brusque rebuke in the daughter's presence stunned my friend. The pain of it was that my husband and I both did love Jesus, but the marriage was broken beyond mending. If she had just put her arms around me and said, 'I'm so sorry . . .'"

Ladies and gentlemen, we have a hugger in the building.[7] If she had just put her arms around you and then what . . . you would have felt better? Look, I'm all for hugging people (with the exception of men's conferences), and as much as I liked Philip's book and loved many of his others, the thing that always bothered me about this story is the lack of details. Forgive me, folks, especially if you have grace, but I believe divorce is generally someone's fault. Sure there are two sides to every story, but one of the stories usually sucks.

Phrases like "the marriage was broken beyond mending" are too vague for me. Did he cheat on you? Sure, then I can understand "broken beyond mending." But if he cheated on you, then you must mean that he loves Jesus now, because he certainly didn't love Jesus when he was cheating on you. If he did love Jesus when he was cheating on you, then this was out of character for him and in a moment of weakness he hurt you in a way that he can never fully understand, but that doesn't constitute "beyond mending," because we all fail at times, and if his past character has been trustworthy and you believe the circumstances behind his momentary lapse of judgment, then there seems to be more room to mend things unless he just habitually cheated on you to the point that you could no longer emotionally endure it.

(Deep breath.)

Philip, why didn't you just tell us what in the heck she meant? Because I gotta be honest, if she's divorcing for reasons other than adultery, child molestation or gross deception, and claims she and her husband both love Jesus, then I'm with the pastor's wife who, although she could use some lessons in tact,[8] was right on by expressing her lack of comprehension regarding this divorce. I don't get it either.

---

7. If you hit any church on the right Sunday, you'll find a lady walking around the foyer offering "free hugs."

8. For further reference see my book *Shut Up! A Comedian's Guide to Tact.*

Now, before you become guilty of showing me a lack of grace because of what I just wrote, let me first say that I highly recommend *What's So Amazing About Grace?* along with numerous other books that highlight God's grace. And I have plenty of grace for troubled marriages, according to my Grace-O-Meter, sold at Christian bookstores everywhere.

I know that some will level the charge of Pharisee, but present-day Pharisees have to do with cultural holiness, which consists of avoiding things such as gambling, drinking, dancing, smoking, charter schools and Smurfs (circa 1985). However, I won't be lampooning judgmental tendencies, because even though this is my Pharisaic downfall, I am blind to it, and the one thing I cannot tolerate is making fun of blind people. Some things are just not funny.

Now, I know some will feel that I have focused too much on marriage, while others will be reading this aloud to their spouses. So here is another example of cockeyed grace. This past year I performed at a music festival with several other comedians. One of my comedy buddies told me, "When I came back to the hotel last night, there was a group of 20 people in the lobby, and they were smashed." (Smashed means drunk for those of you who were homeschooled.)[9] My buddy asked the folks where they were from, and they said, "Oh, we just came from the Christian music festival." I think I can safely make this generalization about Christian music festivals, but groups of drunken pagans don't usually flock to them to get their fill of the News Boys. These are generally Christian folk. But after having seen the News Boys headline the same festival for the last decade, I can at least understand why they might have been drinking. *Can no other group afford a light show?*

---

9. Home schooled = sheltered = innocent = preferable to a jaded 15-year-old.

Let me just say that, personally, I'm not against Christians having an alcoholic beverage now and then. The Bible doesn't say, "Don't drink wine," but it does say pretty clearly, "Don't be drunk." Maybe some Christian music festival should place that banner above the main stage: "Don't be drunk with wine."

In an effort to contrast these two mindsets—the Cheap Grace Mindset vs. the Pharisaic Mindset—I searched the Internet and found an article written by a well-respected Christian financial advisor, who I'm hoping isn't going to put a damper on our Outreach Poker nights.

After browsing the article (because that's what you do on the Internet) and scanning others (because that's what you do with a thesaurus, you find other words for browsing), I've found that most of the arguments against gambling have to do with this slippery slope idea that gambling is a road that leads to bankruptcy, suicide, broken marriages, prostitution and drugs. This is probably why it's so popular. Clearly the message of such a list is, "You're just not safe with poker." UNO, on the other hand, only leads to bad haircuts, Grape Shasta and involuntary celibacy.

Honestly, there is not a verse in the Bible you can point to that says that "gambling is forbidden." Buying and flipping a home is more of a gamble than a $5-per-person-play-for-the-pot poker night. But that's just me. "Do not allow what you consider good to be spoken of as evil" (Rom. 14:16).

I mentioned our Outreach Poker night to a local church Pharisee and he actually said, "Yeah, I should do heroin as an outreach."

"No, but smoking a joint probably wouldn't hurt you."

Straight face. Humor undetected.

"Now, let me get this straight," I said. "You're comparing playing poker to doing heroin?"

As you can see, in this situation, it appears that I am of the cheap-grace crowd. My personality seems to be split between

Pharisee and Cheap Grace: divorce = Pharisee; poker = Cheap Grace. I guess most of us are both Pharisees and Cheap Gracers in varying degrees. Look, I love the ragamuffin trend as much as everyone else, but even popular evangelical trends need correctives or at least rehab, especially if your view of grace has allowed you to become a binging alcoholic. (Based on a true story.)

Regardless of being saved by grace through faith alone, nowhere does the New Testament separate faith from behavior (shout out to all my Catholic friends). As a matter of fact, in that little epistle that the apostle John wrote to Christians to give them assurance of their salvation, one of the assurances he gives them *is* their behavior (see 1 John 2:3-6; 3:16-20).[10] Now, the apostle Paul nicely balances this truth by explaining that you can have all the right behavior and not be motivated in the least bit by love (see 1 Cor. 13:1-2). He says that good behavior without love only makes you a really loud Christian. (And I'm usually plenty loud—I have a microphone.)

All I'm asking you to do is read this, consider it, mull it over, think, pray, wrestle, fear, tremble, work it out, run, jump, sit up and throw a softball. Here's what the apostle John (the Apostle of Love, even) says about the assurance of our salvation: "By this we know that we have come to know Him, *if we keep His commandments*. The one who says, 'I have come to know Him,' and does not keep His commandments, is a liar, and the truth is not in him; but whoever keeps His word, in him the love of God has truly been perfected. By this we know that we are in Him: the one who says he abides in Him ought himself to walk in the same manner as He walked" (1 John 2:3-6, *NASB*, emphasis added. Cool, I finally got to legitimately add emphasis).

Once again, it's those simple uncomplicated followers of Jesus from 2,000 years ago who show us thoughtful Emergent

---

10. My thanks to David Kirkwood for his fine teaching on this subject.

believers the way. John's not saying you're saved by the commandments of Christ; he's just saying that keeping them is evidence that you really are a Christian, a *follower* of Jesus. This is
not about perfection. It's not about trying harder and following
the letter of the law. It's about getting up each day and believing
the right things about grace instead of the wrong things. That
grace is there to *help* us in our time of need, not excuse us. It
doesn't mean that we don't stumble. It just means that we don't
get up every day with the presumption that we can do whatever
we want because we're saved by grace. At least that's what the
note on the refrigerator said (signed by my wife).

Generally, when you believe something, you act on it. Your
actions tell the truth about what you really believe. This is why
you can't berate your wife one moment and tell her you love her
the next. (Sorry about that, honey.) She knows what's in your
heart by how you treat her. She knows if you're showing her
grace. Some of this is just common sense. I've never even been
to a Promise Keepers event.

Maybe we should add a little aside to our benedictions: "May
the Lord bless—actions speak louder than words—and keep you."

Grace comes to the humble, not to the presumptuous (see
1 Pet. 5:5).

During the 1950s, there was a revival of religion on the Isle
of Lewis, which is part of Scotland, which is famous for invisible tape. One of the converts in this revival[11] tells the story of
how one night she was trying to justify herself while listening
to a preacher. She said to herself, "Well, I do pray."

The preacher then asked the crowd, "What do you pray for?"
She said to herself, "I pray that God would make me good."
Then he asked, "For God to make you good?"

---

11. I don't know how others define revival, but what I mean by revival is a manifest
presence of God that is so strong that everyone in the room knows that God is in
this place. During revival, God becomes real.

She sat stunned.

He continued, "If God could make you good, then there was no need for Christ Jesus to come to this earth and die for you. He will not answer it."[12]

It was there, at the end of her self-righteousness, that she found brokenness. That is when grace comes. Grace means that you get saved in spite of you. When you feel like a lousy human being and you bow your head to pray about being a lousy human being and find that God is there after all, that's grace. It comes when you know that you have no other means but Christ alone. Paradoxically, when you know that you can't be good, God provides His power, and you are transformed internally, which goes a long way in how you act. When you know that you cannot be good, God makes a way for you.

And that way is His Spirit inside of you.

Following, living, doing. Now that takes grace.

I hope you're full of it.

---

12. The preacher who said this was Duncan Campbell. You can hear the eyewitnesses to this revival at www.sermonindex.com under the title "Lewis Land of Revival."

CHAPTER 12

In Defense of Uptight

(Calming Your Fears About Fundamentalist Christians)

We're going to end up in the streets.

This is what my mother said soon after my dad died, but you probably didn't know that, because she didn't use quotation marks.

After my father gave up the ghost, my mother, ever the worrier, decided that we were about to go bankrupt because ghosts no longer receive paychecks. My mother handled this crisis like a pro. (Whenever she is confronted with a crisis, she closes her eyes, takes a deep breath and panics.) What I meant by "pro" is that she handled it like a professional crazy person. Also, she taught me that the curtains should always match the couch, and death and bankruptcy seemed to go nicely together.

I have no idea how we will pay the mortgage.

"We? I'm 11. Worry with someone older. And start using quotation marks."

"She went crazy with worry," I think is how the people at the clinic put it. She nearly convinced me that poorhouses still existed and that if we couldn't pay our mortgage, we'd soon have to begin speaking with English accents and cut the fingertips off all our gloves.

This is how the mentally challenged ended up living in our home. Because my mother was nuts. For a monthly fee, she discovered that the state would pay her to let mentally handicapped people live with us. She inquired, but they assured her that she would not be monetarily compensated for letting *me* live with her. "He's not retarded; he's just slow," I think is what the social worker said.

This is pretty devastating to an 11-year-old kid, when your house becomes known as "the house where the retards live." I just wish kids weren't saying this before the mentally challenged girls moved in.

Debbie. I remember Debbie. She had a light case of Down's syndrome, which probably isn't an official diagnosis. I realize that's kind of like saying, "He was pretty handsome for an ugly fella." Mentally, she was 11, with a bigger butt. Physically, she was 16, with a bigger butt.

Secretly, I liked having Debbie around. She was mentally astute enough to play checkers and other board games without eating any of the pieces. Since I was the youngest in my family—everyone had moved out of the house—Down's syndrome-lite Debbie was the closest thing I had to a sibling then.

But, of course, I couldn't be seen with a "retard" in public.

And this brings me to the subject of this chapter: fundamentalist Christians. No one wants to be seen in public with them anymore, but if we're all honest—and by all, I mean evangelicals, emerging church planters, Fuller seminary graduates and the mentally challenged in general—we owe our faith to such as these. It was their simple explanation of the gospel that got most of us where we are today—in a deep spiritual depression that we just can't shake. Seriously, if it weren't for them, we wouldn't be who we are—Christians making fun of them from a distance.

I remember when I felt I had to make fun of Debbie in front of the neighborhood kids to disassociate myself from her, later apologizing in private so that we could play checkers. That's why I've decided to defend the fundamentalists in this chapter, because Debbie always ended up playing checkers with me even though I made fun of her. She may have been retarded, but she had a better heart than I did. And the heart is the thing to look at when you're listening to anyone—figuratively, of course.

Most evangelical and Emergent Christians want to distance themselves from fundamentalist Christians in general and from religion in particular.

Christians have this thing about being called religious. They don't like it, which I don't really understand, because I never used to be religious. There are two things most Christians don't want to be called, three to be sure: fundamentalist, religious, or worst of all, religious fundamentalist.

I did not grow up in a Christian home—our builders were pagans. Actually, I didn't even know what the resurrection of Christ was until I was a freshman in college. But I was always in the slow reading group, which only added to the stigma of having retarded girls living in the home. I don't know if slow reading groups even exist today, but before the term "middle school" caught on, there were separate reading groups based on how fast you could read. Those of us who couldn't read fast were called slow, literally. I didn't mind. It was certainly better than calling us dumb readers, which is what a lot of the kids at school called us.

That's something that being in the slow reading group and having mentally challenged girls living with us taught me: People are concerned about what you call them and about what group you associate them with. When I first became a follower of Jesus, other Christians often corrected me when I used the word "religious" to describe myself or other Christians. They would say things like, "I'm not religious. I'm a Christian."

"Really? I'm not retarded. I'm slow."

It's confusing stuff for a new believer, but I've come to understand that Christians want the name Christian to mean something other than "a rightwing nutcase." They don't like being called religious, I imagine, because much like the word "eggs" is commonly associated with "bacon," as in bacon and eggs, the word "religious" is most commonly associated with "hypocrites," as in hypocrites and eggs.

The other thing Christians who hate the word "religious" are really trying to do is distinguish what type of Christian they are, such as the born-again variety. Misconceptions about what it means to be a born-again Christian still persist. It's pretty simple really. You just bow your head, say a simple prayer and when you open your eyes—you're a registered Republican with a firearm. The process is made even simpler when churches leave out repentance.

Not only do we fret over what to call ourselves, but believe it or not, my people (Christians) struggle with what to call you people—pagans, heathens, hedonists, atheists, home builders. Whatever you happen to be, please choose your own label and add "postmodern" to the beginning of it.

We've toyed with terms such as "unchurched" (a made-up word that sounds more like a Lutheran who's been deprogrammed), "pre-Christian" (back when church was sometimes cancelled due to dinosaurs during the prehistoric era), "non-Christian" (too much like a Starbucks order—"I'll have an iced chai tea non-fat non-Christian"), "unbeliever" (too political, assuming that it means United Nations believer), "unsaved" (too mean), "sinner" (too obvious), "jackass" (too honest).

I don't know what to call you either, so I'll just call you "reader." That way, whether you're a Christian or not, you can still be a reader.

Still, I wouldn't mind seeing a Bible translation using the word "jackass": "For God demonstrated his own love toward us in that while we were yet jackasses, Christ died for us" (Rom. 5:8).

You can call us jackasses, but whatever you do, don't call us religious.

We just don't like the word "religious."

Christians who have an issue with being called religious say things like, "I hate religion, but I love Jesus." They also say things like, "Religion is about dead rituals," if by dead rituals you mean Catholics. They never use the phrase "dead rituals" in reference to Lutherans. They just use the word "boring."

Why do some Christians fear the word "religious"? Any library-worn *Webster's* dictionary defines it as "believing in or showing devotion for a deity." That's what all followers of Jesus do even today, including Catholics and Lutherans. Maybe more Christians should use a dictionary once in a while. Still, I've noticed that there are groups of Christians who hate religious people, meaning other followers of Jesus who are, well, religious about it—Christians who aren't bright enough to embrace the trendiest forms of doubt.

Something I've observed—and I base this non-empirical evidence on two whole people I know—is that some people who grow up in fundamentalism end up hating people they consider religious. Maybe "hate" is not the word they would use. Despise. They despise them. I assume.

The two people I've noticed this from I will call Phil and Don. Each grew up in some type of Christian home and each of them has deep-seated problems with fundamentalist Christians and religious types. Since I have a six-year-old daughter who is growing up in a Christian home, this scares the crap out of me. But at least my two examples have still followed Jesus. It's at least comforting to know that my daughter will still follow Jesus while despising most of Christendom.

Personally, I don't get offended when someone refers to me as "very religious." At least they've noticed there's something going on with me spiritually. If people call you "stinky," now that's something to be concerned about.

I like really religious people, but sadly they do not often like me. I'm finding that it doesn't matter what a person believes, everyone is offended by body odor (or a generally obnoxious comedian with the nickname Stinky).

I'm pretty sure that Hank Hanegraaff doesn't like me, even though he probably doesn't remember not liking me. Hank hosts a national radio program called *The Bible Answer Man*, where he answers questions daily about why people shouldn't fall down in church when someone prays for them.

> **Hank**: Is the caller there?
> **Caller**: Yes, Hank, I'm a big fan. I was reading this book that talks about God giving people dreams and—
> **Hank**: It's dangerous. Stay away. Don't fall down. Next caller.
> **Caller #2**: Hank, I was wondering—
> **Hank**: Dangerous! There's danger in wondering! Stop wondering before someone hypnotizes you.

As a comedian for hire, I was commissioned to do a show for a group of elite members (like there are any other kind) of the National Religious Broadcasters. There were about 30 of them, and the gig was on a lunch cruise ship, which is a cruise ship that takes a group out for half a day, feeds them lunch and returns them to shore. It's like a vacation for busy people.

There I was, trapped on a boat with some of the most conservative minds in fundamentalism. Naturally, I was tempted to sink the boat.[1]

The lady in charge of the event, who was really very nice, said to me, "Now, you understand that the group on this cruise is very, very conservative?"

---

1. I would never intentionally sink a boat full of fundamentalists or any other kind of Christian group. I'm not that good of a swimmer.

"Yeah, I kind of picked up on that about the third time you mentioned it."

Plus the guy wearing a Speedo over his pinstripe suit gave me the idea—hey, he might be a little conservative.

She was probably concerned, based on the reputation of comedians, about what I would say during my show.

The lady in charge of the NRB lunch cruise gave me a nice introduction that began with, "Does anyone else smell that? I think it's body odor." Then I performed my little show for a group of ultra-conservative Christians who responded like a group of ultra-conservative Christians. They laughed in all the right places, but not like a black gospel church crowd would laugh. No one stood up to smack his leg during my literal boat act.[2] They were gracious but rarely emotional, and many were preoccupied with avoiding dangerous doctrines.

Then it happened. About five minutes into my set, Hank, who was sitting near the back, got up and walked out to the ship deck, obviously driven to suicide by my act. He leaned on the railing and just stared at the ocean with a longing that I was at the bottom. (I assume.) What was going through the Bible-prism of his mind? He was probably out there praying, "Oh, Lord, what has become of Your Church? They're sending jesters to us now, like this is a time to laugh. Please, God, send a big fish to swallow *and* digest him."

Honestly, I didn't take it personally. I mean, if we're truly honest, most of us are embarrassed to be seen in public with a retarded person.

In a 2005 *Rolling Stone* interview, Bono explained his embarrassment of religious fundamentalism:

---

2. In the subculture of comedy, the pejorative term "boat act" refers to the type of variety comedy acts that appeal to cruise lines, such as jugglers, magicians, unicycle-riding guitar players, etc. (The type of acts most of us would be if we were more talented.)

So now—cut to 1980. Irish rock group, who've been through the fire of a certain kind of revival, a Christian-type revival, go to America. Turn on the TV the night you arrive, and there's all these people talking from the Scriptures. But they're quite obviously raving lunatics.

Suddenly you go, what's this? And you change the channel, and there's another secondhand-car salesman. You think, oh, my God. But their words sound so similar . . . to the words out of *our* mouths.

So what happens? You learn to shut up. You say, whoa, what's this going on? You go oddly still and quiet. If you talk like this around here, people will think you're one of those.

Therein lies the inherent fear of being "religious"—we don't want to become "one of those." Not that we give credence to the theological leanings of a rock star. You might as well get your theological views from a comedian.

We're all embarrassed by someone.

For example, popular Bible teacher and author John McArthur believes that Charismatic Christians, the ones who are so fundamentalist that they believe in the gifts of the Spirit, like healing and Mercedes-Benzes, are dangerous, which is ludicrous because Charismatic Christians are too silly to be dangerous. But they're still Christians. They just bounce a lot. They're like fundamentalist Tiggers.

Not believing that the gifts of the Spirit are active today is just as silly as believing that Charismatic Christians are dangerous. To many younger evangelicals, this fear of spiritual experiences, especially biblically based ones, is silly. I find it tremendously silly that there are Bible colleges that forbid speaking in tongues, which has always confused me. How do you ban something that's *in* the Bible? I would love to attend this school's orientation. "It's against school policy to hold up your hands while praying, speak in tongues or walk on water. These things should be avoided at all cost and reported immediately when observed, because it's not against school policy to tattle."

That's just modernity run amok.

There has always been a tendency in the American Church to distance themselves (I include myself) from the brands of American Christian faith that are not theirs. "I'm not one of those. I can't believe [Insert Name of Nationally Known Crazy Evangelist] said that, either. Look, I'm a Christian, but I'm not that kind of Christian. I'm the new kind."

We all have our prejudices.

I have to admit that when someone tells me they went to Oral Roberts University, I always want to ask, "Why would you do that?" I figure if he seems nuts to me, it should be obvious to everyone. Things are not always so. People need help knowing who's nuts and who's not. I'm here to help, just like Hank.

I have a niece who is one year older than I am. Assume all you like about my family history and you'll probably be close to the truth. She was traveling with a band, playing bars and clubs around the country, when one night in her hotel room she flipped on the television and Pat Robertson of *The 700 Club* popped up on the screen. In all honesty, the first time she told me she got saved by watching Pat Robertson, I was more than a little disappointed. I wanted her to become a Christian via a more reputable means, you know, like a Christian comedian.

But God used Pat Robertson.

Now, Pat Robertson and Hank Hanegraaff are definitely different Christian brands, much like classic Coke and Shasta's Wildberry Revival Fruit Drink are different brands. If you can get Pat and Hank to sit at the same table, call me and I will perform at that event gratis, provided there is plenty of Revival

Fruit Drink. Still, they can both be classified as very religious, and they probably agree on the fundamentals of the faith; so they could even be called fundamentalists, along with John McArthur, who's more of a Sunsweet Prune Juice, not from concentrate, of course.

The thing I really like about these religious fundamentalists is that they sincerely want to get the work of the Kingdom done. They want people to come to know Christ. They believe in the urgency of life. They understand the danger of false beliefs. They don't care if their views are unfashionable or unpopular. They care about the Truth, about making Jesus known.

Now, I don't personally know John or Hank or Pat, but it's what I believe about them. And that's why these religious fundamentalists don't bother me. It's because of people like them that I "got saved." I ended up in a different Christian camp, drinking another beverage, Pixy Stix Emergent Fizz Soda, but they brought me to the Savior. Not John or Hank or Pat personally, but people like them. That's why I like radical followers of Jesus who don't care what people think. They just dust off their shoes, stab a straw into their Capri Sun, and move to the next house.

I have some friends who can certainly be classified as fundamentalist Christians. These friends won't watch certain movies or listen to certain music or mingle with charter school moms. They're trying to curb their badness or at least keep it under control. They're very religious about their Christianity. This is probably why they appear too holy, or what many people today refer to as "uptight."

People who aren't uptight often fail to see the benefits that uptight people bring to our society. Hugh Hefner will readily admit that if elements of our society weren't repressed, his *Playboy* magazine would have never become successful. It was a naughty magazine, making adults in the 1950s snicker like little children. And this in no way endorses *Playboy* magazine, because I am still amazed when I see TV bios that treat Hefner like he is some sort of sophisticate, walking around in a velvet pajama coat, sucking on a cigarette holder, the parody of a sophisticate. Or when Larry Flint is hailed as some champion of freedom of speech. Listen, I've seen *Hustler* magazine and there's really no speech involved, but I understand what they're trying to say.

All I'm saying is that you shameless business people (aka HBO executives) owe the success of naughty to the prudes of society. It's just something for you to think about the next time you talk about how much you fear religious fundamentalists. You owe your success to such as these. What's better free publicity for a book or a movie than some national boycott or protest? That's why this country needs obnoxiously religious people. It's a checks and balances thing. Think about it, folks. That nagging little religious person in your life may be the only reason you haven't become the raging alcoholic that you truly are. Instead of downing that bottle of Jack, you just had a couple of beers.

Way to go, religious people.

When I was a kid, I'd get mad during the Christmas season when people tried to insert all this Jesus stuff into the holiday. "Jesus? What's He got to do with Christmas? He doesn't have anything to do with Santa and gifts and elves."

"*The Little Drummer Boy*'s on."

Boring.

Give me Rudolph and Frosty or that puppet version of Fred Astair.

As an eight-year-old, I was passionate about *not* having Jesus as part of the holiday season. Now that I've met the risen Savior, I have to confess—I'm pretty religious about this whole Christian thing.

Like it or not, John McArthur, me and Pat's all brothers, y'all. Donald Miller and the Bible Answer Man? Mansion Room-

ies. Philip Yancey and Jerry Falwell, kin. Leonard Ravenhill and
Brian McLaren . . . only God knows. There's a cycle of influence
in this community of faith that we cannot escape. Fundamentalists get us saved, and then we thirst and get baptized in the
Spirit and speak in tongues and soon tire of anti-intellectual
excesses and discover Donald Miller's poetic authenticity and
Brian McLaren's loving challenges, but soon tire of the relent-
less doubt of postmodernism, so we return to the fundamentals of the faith and write honestly about the fundamentalists
and, in essence, defend them.

It's just part of being religious, I guess.

In addition to attending Mark Driscoll's church online, I often
download sermons from this website called SermonIndex.com,
where they have thousands of sermons from old-school fundamentalist preachers, meaning lots of dead guys. One night the
featured sermon was some preacher from South Africa who
was a contemporary, meaning not dead yet, but still old-time in
his preaching style, delivering what turned out to be more of
a rambling stream-of-consciousness message that was called
"A Warning to America," with a 20-minute aside on the dangers
of rock and roll, a viewpoint that loses credibility when you're
under 70. Setting aside his unfounded diatribe against rock
and roll, I discovered a beautiful heart, a heart that loved God
and openly wept over the shamelessness of some of New York
City's neon porn.

One of his dreams was to bring his wife and children to see
New York City, but when he found himself alone on the streets
of Times Square confronted by several buildings of indescribable indecency—which I would like to describe in detail but I've
already said they're indescribable—he experienced what some
might call culture shock but others might call righteous
indignation. You couldn't walk a block without running into a
drug dealer or a hooker or a peep show, which, of course, was

very convenient for people looking for that sort of thing. Looking at the crowds on the streets, filled with island natives and many tourists with children in tow, what I love about this old guy is that he began to weep and pray aloud right there on the street, asking God over and over to "close these buildings down, Lord! They're defiling the children! I can't bring my family here. Close these buildings down!"

Not knowing how long he actually prayed, he opened his eyes and found himself surrounded by several hundred people, many who were crying themselves. No, the *Letterman Show* wasn't cancelled. That's not why they were crying. His prayers actually attracted a crowd.

Let us have a moment of silence now for people who are embarrassed to pray in public.

Yeah, I know that some of you will find this too farfetched to believe. Jonah couldn't have been swallowed by a whale; water doesn't just part; and people on the streets of New York City don't cry at praying strangers.

This old-time South African missionary fundamentalist said that three months later he was back in New York, stopping at a coffee shop where he bought a paper. The headline told of the mayor's threat to close these buildings down, which he did shortly thereafter.

This old preacher's faith is simple, fundamentalist and effective. "The prayer of a righteous man is powerful and effective" (Jas. 5:16). It's a most true proposition. His views on rock and roll are certainly retarded, but he has a better heart than I do. I owe not only my faith but often my continued growth in grace to people like him—people who challenge and provoke me and who are rejected by the evangelical church at large. People who make Christians feel like sinners—unrighteous, unholy, ungodly, things we don't feel nearly often enough.

We're not troubled by the sins of society anymore.

There is no shame.

If it wasn't for fundamentalist Christians, who would act as the antithesis for the freight train of shamelessness that is speeding through our cities? We need these fundamentalist Christians around, especially since the statistics say that only 7 percent of evangelical Christians share their faith on a regular basis. Somebody has to do it.

That leaves the fundamentalists.

CHAPTER 13

Everybody Likes Jesus

(Christology, Which Is Christ with -ology Added to His Name)

My first experience with Jesus came at age 11, when my parents went to Rochester, Minnesota, to see if my dad could have open-heart surgery. The Mayo Clinic in Minnesota is famous for extending lives, partly due to the fact that your lifespan is twice as long if you're frozen half the year. Minnesota is the only state I've ever been to where you can get an ice-cream headache from breathing.

While my parents were away, I stayed with some relatives. Now, having grown up in a nominally Christian home, we attended church just enough to learn some bedtime prayers, to keep the Jehovah's Witnesses at bay and to feel guilty about sex, but not enough to find out about the Resurrection. One of the prayers I learned during this time was that morbid "if I should die" prayer. You may know how it goes: "Now I lay me down to sleep, I pray the Lord my soul to keep," which is a great prayer to teach your kids. "If I should die before I wake—Goodnight, Timmy. Hope you're alive in the morning. Hope the Lord doesn't come back and get you in the middle of the night. Don't let the bedbugs bite. Yeah, there're bugs in your bed and they're gonna bite you all night. If the Lord doesn't come back and get ya, the bugs are gonna bite ya. You got no chance, Timmy. Just stay up."

I don't know why my parents called me Timmy.

Anyway, that night I said my bedtime prayers as usual, because I had eaten something my sister had cooked, who, after all, was infamous for making grilled cheese sandwiches but forgetting the cheese (something most people call toast). Then I said a little prayer for my dad, which was very unusual because he didn't even like grilled cheese. The next morning I awoke, and the only way I can describe it is that the presence of Christ was there in a way that I knew that I knew that I knew that Jesus loved me. Now, don't misunderstand me, I'm not saying that Christ appeared to me physically or anything, he wasn't even 900 feet tall.[1] All I'm saying is that I awoke to an invisible presence, but I knew that presence was the Person of Jesus Christ. At least, that's what the side effects to my cold medicine said.

Seriously, for the moment anyway, as an 11-year-old boy, I knelt by my bed for the first time in my life and told Jesus that I loved Him. In effect, I was only responding to this overwhelming presence of love. The apostle John wrote, in the short letter of 1 John, that the only reason we love God is because God first loved us (see 1 John 4:19). It was just real that day. For whatever reason, God revealed His love to me.

So, naturally, I ignored Him for 20 years.

I don't remember the particulars of the day, but I do remember walking home from school with a peace that I haven't had to this day. As I said, I was 11 when this occurred; soon after I entered puberty, discovered girls and that was the end of that.

I like girls.

Goodnight.

---

1. "If you didn't catch that reference, in the 1980s, televangelist Oral Roberts had a vision of a 900-foot-tall Jesus (300-meter Jesus in Europe), because a 90-foot-tall Jesus is just not that impressive, and a 9-foot-tall Nazarene would just be a basketball player." I discovered this footnote on the Web while trying to verify the actual height of Oral Roberts's vision and stumbled upon this explanation, which I thought was very funny. I have no idea who to credit for it, though it could possibly be a site called www.captainwacky.com.

Eventually, I dismissed what happened to me as an emotional experience, much like watching the ending of *West Side Story* where the white kids are having trouble picking up Tony's body; when a Puerto Rican kid helps them, you burst into such a loud wail that you frighten your family. I believed that Christianity was nothing more than an emotional reaction to certain psychological stimuli, but Christians were just too dumb to grow past this. *Evolve, people.*

As a freshman in high school, I remember walking home from school and berating one of my friends for his Catholic faith. I don't remember exactly what I said to him, but it boiled down to *you're dumb*. It was just self-righteousness on my part, the same emotion people exhibit when they snap at the Starbucks barista for getting their order wrong. *How dare you delay the Lord of Mocha!*[2] It's the same emotion the people in the suburbs are unaware they're feeling when they wish the homeless people in their local parks would go away. People think that only religious people are self-righteous. Baby, anyone who doesn't need a Savior is self-righteous. Jesus even said He didn't come for the righteous, for those who feel all right within themselves (see Matt. 9:13). He came for the unrighteous, for people in customer service everywhere.

Oddly enough, even though I felt this way at the time, I'd never actually read the New Testament. So, I had little basis on which to judge my experience either way.

But that is the question.

What does it truly mean to encounter Jesus?

Anne Lamott, Little Richard, Jane Fonda, Bob Dylan and B. J. Thomas all encountered Jesus. Heck, even my mother-in-law's been slain in the Spirit, to no avail. Anne Lamott, Buddhist-type

---

2. Mark Driscoll once said that anything good he says, he's stolen. Just returning the favor.

Christian leftist, sophisticated bag lady of sorts, President of Confusion and a wonderful writer, describes a very real experience with Jesus in her book *Traveling Mercies*. When I first picked up her book, without ever having heard of her, about halfway through it I said to my wife, "I've found my new best friend." After finishing her book, I realized that my new best friend is nuts. Anne is Jesus-y, but she's not orthodoxy. Nevertheless, I still read all her books, because she has a great sense of humor about things. I'm not dismissing her experience, only her theology.

The issue is significant because all of these people claim to have encountered the Jesus of the Bible; but whether or not they were given a "new believer's packet," we are not sure. In short, if we don't have a way of processing our encounters with Christ, besides our own burning in the bosom, we could end up with a Jesus as imaginary friend, not the real Jesus.

One of the problems we have with interpreting the Jesus of the Bible, after hundreds of years and innumerable Christian leaders have commented and written and preached and emphasized differing aspects of the Gospels, only later to be caught with the church secretary, is bowing our own feelings to the Scriptures. The Jesus of experience is meaningless without the Jesus of the Bible. The Jesus of experience is made your servant without your submission to the words in red.

Alan Redpath, British preacher and one-time pastor of Chicago's Moody Bible Church, once said, "The early church's theology was based on their experience. It was doxology before it was theology. Now we have plenty of theology but little experience." Then the National Association of Evangelicals drowned him, a little something we call Extreme Baptism. Consequently, the two extremes to avoid are theology without experience and experience with little theology (shout out to all my Charismatic friends). Our experience needs to be interpreted by our theology or we end up with a Jesus-y feel-good mist that demands nothing and offends no one—not that the emerging church hasn't influenced evangelicalism in positive ways too.

The emerging church likes Jesus.

But then again, everybody likes Jesus.

You don't find too many people who are complaining, "I've had it with this Jesus character. Feed the poor, love your neighbor, vote Republican! What is it with that guy?" Generally, people don't complain about Jesus, which is odd because Jesus holds the opinion that people hate Him (see John 7:7). Where did He get that idea? (Besides the crucifixion thing.) Jesus has always maintained that the majority just won't get Him (see Matt. 7:14)—which may explain why the Republicans keep winning—and that deep down, below the cockles of their belly fat, they really hate Him. Jesus said that some will hate Him without reason (see John 15:25), while others will see miracles and still hate Him (see John 15:24). He promises His followers that they will be hated by all nations (see Matt. 24:9) and tells them to keep in mind that if the world hates you, it hated Him first (see John 15:18). *Quick, where do I sign up?*

Even the Church is full of people who actually hate Jesus (see Matt. 7:23; Titus 1:16). Oh, they say they love Jesus and sing and raise their hands and eat macaroni salad (the Early Church's communion backup plan). But it's obvious that they hate Jesus by how they treat their neighbor, who is Jesus in disguise,[3] just like in the movie *Bruce Almighty*, which I hesitate mentioning because we've become so theologically shallow that many sincere Christians think this movie is deep. But then again, in the Charismatic community, *The Matrix* was a prophetic word from the Lord.

---

3. Think about that, Church. The next time you want to spit at a parade of gays marching with banners, you are actually spitting at Jesus. If you berate a woman walking into an abortion clinic, you're berating Jesus. This isn't to say you can't speak the truth, but don't let your righteous anger compel you to unrighteous behavior. Shame, shame.

People like the idea of Jesus but not the reality of Jesus. The same way people like the idea of feeding the poor but not *really* feeding the poor. Generally, we prefer to work among the poor with our MasterCard. *If they can deduct $30 a month from our cards to feed a child, can't they find someone else to hand him the food? We've done our part, don't ya think?*

Much of the dilemma that the emerging church is dealing with is based on questions like, Why aren't more people following Jesus? Why are we losing our young people? Can mall security help us find them? Thus, they diagnose the problem as modernity, irrelevancy or church mime groups, then devise solutions, just as the baby boomers did several generations ago and came up with the answers of rock music and goatees. My diagnosis is that people don't follow Jesus in any generation because they don't really like Him (see John 14:23).

But, why?

Why don't people like Jesus?

People like the idea of Jesus, which is much different than liking Jesus. They usually hate it when the idea becomes tangible. If you became a Christian in college, this is certainly something you understand from experience, like the weekend you came home and broke the news to your parents, "I became a Christian." Many times this news is met with dismay, anger, resentment or your mother crying, "Why couldn't you have just been gay?"

When I came to experience Christ as a freshman in college—thankfully, I attended the same college as my Savior—it was through a lecture on evidences for the resurrection of Christ. Here I was, a freshman in college with a nominal church background, making it on big game days like Christmas and Easter and the two-a-days of vacation Bible school, yet I had never heard that Jesus had risen from the dead. I didn't know that was the cornerstone of the Christian faith. Right away, I called our old pastor, "You know what this guy did? You think you might have mentioned that? It's just something for you to consider. Next time you're preaching, you might wanna throw in that little tidbit."

When you speak of experiencing Christ, it's really important to mention the Resurrection. He rose from the dead, and that is why we can experience Him now. As it turns out, it has nothing to do with prescription drugs.

My experience of Christ compares to the Gospel stories of Christ in the sense that during His earthly ministry people were drawn to Jesus, some for His miracles, some for His teaching, some for the all-you-can-eat buffets; but many were also drawn just for His presence, just to be around Him. (Not to mention that little turning-water-into-wine thingy. That'll always draw a crowd.)

Jesus Christ, when walking the earth, undoubtedly had a presence that no other living being has ever had: God is love, and there He is in the flesh. That is why Jesus can tell you the truth about yourself, and though it hurts, it melts you at the same time. Love can speak like nothing else. That's why many of us can say something that is true spiritually, but it falls flat or only bangs the gong, because we are not love personified. We're not even love hinted at—we're just big loud truth gongs, not that I don't have a good relationship with my mother-in-law.[4]

Looking back, I believe now that my experience with Jesus was legitimate. For whatever reason, Jesus told me He loved me, and it has hung over my life like the perfect cloud. I didn't understand the gospel at the time, but through no goodness of my own, God put His mark on me. It's just I'm a slow learner.

---

4. The Bible says to honor your father and mother. It says nothing about your mother-in-law. This is because God never gives us more than we can handle.

My apologies to Starbucks baristas across the nation.

When Paul tells Christians to speak the truth in love, he is in essence saying, "Speak the truth with the presence of Christ," which would also entail speaking the truth with holiness and mercy and all the other things that make up the Person of Christ. This is a tall order. As many biblical scholars have noted, "Just give up now." I guess the apostles believed that the Church was capable of obeying Christ through the empowering of the Holy Spirit. Too bad more Christians don't. We just point to Romans 7 and claim that Paul would have stumbled over the same women at the mall.

Personally, I believe that the actual manifest presence of Christ is starkly missing from the Church at large, if I may make an unsubstantiated and sweeping generalization for the sake of my point. Besides, I walked down the street to our local coffee shop where three people there agreed with me, so this certainly makes it a national phenomenon.

During our discussion of Jesus at our theology group one night, the subject of praying to Jesus was introduced, not that we would actually consider praying together, but we talked about it just the same. That's what you do at a theology group. You talk about things you should do, but don't. It was a rather depressing chat, I must confess, because we all came to the conclusion that in America, we don't really need Jesus. What I mean is that we don't need to pray for our daily bread because our cupboards are full. Even poor people are fat in America. We don't need to cry out for healing because we have great medical care. Anyone with enough cash flow can launch a church and see growth just like a good business. We don't desperately need the presence of Christ to help our programs function and get our budgets met. Honestly, we don't really thirst for the presence of Christ.

Another round of Amstel Light, please.

There once was a missionary who was missioneering—which is like Imagineering, except the natives are not automatrons[5]— somewhere far, far away in the pagan world in such a remote location that he literally had to pray daily for his food, not to give thanks for it but to actually get some. Each day that he had food was a miracle. When he came back to the States, he said it was the thing he missed the most, seeing God's daily care and provision in small but miraculous ways. Punching buttons on the microwave and then shouting "It's a miracle" when it beeps isn't quite the same.

When it comes to experiencing Jesus in people, nearly everyone will fail you. This is why books are so great. They're the thoughts of people without all the mess. During college, I read so many books on Christianity that my grades suffered. "Professor, I'm sure that biology is important, but how important is understanding your body if your soul ends up in hell?"

Class dismissed.

I remember reading this short book by Francis Schaeffer called *The Mark of a Christian*. It was a turning point in my life. Unfortunately, I missed the turn. In his book, Schaeffer, an influential Christian thinker in his day, said the cause of Christ suffered because the mark of a Christian should be love. This, he contended, was not the image of Christians that the world at large sees. I remember thinking, *This should be the book I base my whole Christian life upon. (Aside from the Bible, of course. And Batman comics.)* But there were competing authors speaking into my life. Charles Finney, an influential thinker in his day, was both a

---

5. I just had an idea. After J. Vernon McGee died, they kept his radio show going, the Energizer Bunny of ministries. They just play his old sermons over and over again. Well, when famous pastors die, such as Jerry Falwell, why not commission Disney to make an automatronic version of the pastor, place it in the pulpit and have the automatron give all his old sermons that are on tape? It's just an idea. I know I'd go hear automatronic Jerry Falwell.

colossal intellect and a man with a passion in his bones that emanated from the pages of his writings. Finney was the original hellfire and brimstone lawyer turned preacher. Imagine, if you will, Sam Harris as an evangelical. Finney's sermons cut me to the core. Schaeffer, in his appeal to the intellectual community, lost out to the more passionate Finney. I wanted both mental and spiritual fire.

Love would have been a better choice.

So, during college, I walked around campus telling the unvarnished truth. In other words, I was a butthead. (I know, I know. Some of you are saying, "You haven't changed much." But even the statement, "If you think he's a butthead now, you should have known him before he got saved," can be a testimony.)

After reading Finney, I even doubted Billy Graham's salvation, so you can imagine how I felt about myself, and others. Naturally, I repented about every 30 seconds. I prayed for at least an hour a day, which lowered my repentance-per-minute rate to 1 rpm (repentance per minute); but this only lasted during the hour of prayer. I shared the gospel with people regularly, even converted one poor college freshman who soon fled my presence in exchange for a Lambda Chi Christian who exhibited some grace, not to mention a secret handshake.

I strove hard to be righteous. As a matter of fact, I strove so hard to be righteous that I was self-righteous. Sincerely righteous people cannot often detect their self-righteousness because they have correct theology. They understand that they're saved by grace, by the "scandal of the cross," but their practice is heresy, as is their experience. The presence of God in my life was null, because God is opposed to the proud, which is what self-righteousness leads to—pride. And if not repented of, it could lead to scandalously published humor books mocking the evangelical subculture and the emerging church's tendency to overuse the word "scandalous" in its many forms.

The thing about comparing our experience of Christ with the Bible is that it isn't limited to only the parts where Jesus talks. The whole Bible alludes to Jesus, even when He's not the one doing the talking. He is the subtext of every essential to the faith. Saved by grace through faith—that's because of Jesus. The inspiration of the Bible—the only place we get the words of Jesus. Jesus as God in the flesh—not just an option but the Supreme Being. Jesus as fully human, which makes Him the most difficult subject to write about, because being fully man and fully God lends itself to being easily misunderstood by people who are fully human and fully moron. We often speak of the Jesus of the Gospels, but buried within the stories of Christ in the Gospels is the preaching of John the Baptist, who preached Christ's coming more fervently than Anne Lamott venting about the Bush administration.

Most people like John the Baptist because he told off religious people, which is why people started saying, "I'm not religious; I'm a Christian." John the Baptist reminded religious leaders to "produce fruit in keeping with repentance," while the crowd of common people looked at each other asking, "Does that mean us too?" Then John said to the leaders, "And do not think you can say to yourselves, 'We have Abraham as our father.' I tell you that out of these stones God can raise up children of Abraham." So, phooey on your traditions. It doesn't matter that the Methodists have a great history of revival. What's happening now in Methodism? Is God moving today? It doesn't matter that Catholicism is home of the Early Church fathers. What is happening now? It doesn't matter how blessed your particular Christian faith tradition began, God can make followers out of stones, which comes as good news to women who've had collagen injections.

John basically says that God will cut down a faith tradition that doesn't produce fruit, making California Presbyterians

who own orange groves falsely secure and street preachers a little nervous. Is it any wonder that some denominations feel
dead? Now, this isn't to say that Church history isn't important, because it's extremely important, and traditions are a
good thing; but don't rest on your laurels is, I think, his point,
because Laurel was the thin one and he can't support your
weight. Sure, rest on your Hardies, but not on your Laurels.
Tee-hee. Hand over mouth.

Then John the Baptist presents a picture of Jesus that most
branches of the Church ignore, whether evangelical, emergent
or mainline. John the Baptist says of Christ, "His winnowing
fork is in his hand, and he will clear his threshing floor, gathering his wheat into the barn and burning up the chaff with
unquenchable fire." Then right after this, Jesus shows up and
says, "I gotta hear this guy preach!" Jesus really liked John the
Baptist, who was a much different communicator than Jesus.
John didn't use parables. He was blunt and fiery, brisk, to the
point. He said things that others were thinking but were afraid
to say. More the tools of the comedian, except that he doesn't
seem to have a sense of humor when he points to Herod's wife and
says, "That chick left her husband and married his brother."

You see? That sentence could use a punch line.

"That chick left her husband and married his brother; this
way, all the wedding gifts stay in the family."

Something to lighten the delivery, to keep his head from
getting chopped off.

The Winnowing Fork Jesus is not a Jesus often spoken of
these days, probably because we don't know what a winnowing fork is. From what I can gather, it's like an ancient com-
bine that's less likely to pull your arm off but more likely to
swipe off your head. With two hands, the agricultural specialist would swipe the wheat into the air with this tool, sometimes smacking a novice farmer in the head who didn't know

to keep his distance. Then the wind would blow away the chaff because it was light. The wheat, which was heavier, would fall to the ground along with the novice farmer's head. Now, this illustration should make shallow believers tremble inside, but it doesn't really, precisely because they are shallow. (Did I say "they"? I meant "we." I'm the one writing a theological humor book.)

The mercy in John's description of Jesus comes from the fact that he says the fork is in Jesus' hand, so it doesn't sound like He has gripped it with both hands yet. Apparently, He's holding it like American Gothic. This clearing of the threshing floor will happen someday but hasn't happened yet, for there He stands: Israelite Gothic.

You can never look at Christ and exclude either His mercy or His judgment. This is the balancing act that we Christians struggle with: Cheap Grace or Pharisee. "*Consider therefore the kindness and sternness of God*" (Rom. 11:22). We need each other to be reminded of it, which is why Cheap Gracers and Pharisees should have more church picnics together.

The conviction that we feel after encountering Jesus is often the Winnowing Fork aspect of Jesus. The Holy Spirit whispering to us, "Stop that."

"But I love her."

"Then stop defiling her."

"Are you saying sex before marriage is wrong?"

"Yes."

"Can I get a second opinion?"

Whenever we experience Jesus, we focus on the loving presence we feel; the acceptance that God shows us in Christ; the Holy Spirit who pours out the love of Christ in our hearts; gentle Jesus, meek and mild. Our tendency is to ignore the other aspects of His revealed personality in the Bible, such as the Jesus of the book of Revelation, who is thus described: "His head and hair were white like wool, as white as snow, and his eyes were like a blazing fire. His feet were like bronze glowing in a furnace, and his voice was like the sound of rushing waters. In his right hand were seven stars, and out of his mouth came a sharp double-edged sword. His face was like a sun shining in all its brilliance" (1:14-16).

Wow! Little baby Jesus is all growed up.

This is the Jesus the apostle John saw, the Christ with fire in His eyes and a sword in His mouth. Then the apostle John shows his intelligence when he writes, "When I saw him, I fell at his feet as though dead." That's really the best way to react to someone who has a sword popping out of His mouth. John was in the presence of Almighty God, and the etiquette for this, if you ever find yourself in such a situation, is to fall down like you're dead. But I imagine it's just an involuntary reaction. When God shows up, you fall down,[6] which is way less embarrassing than peeing your pants.

Then we find a completely frightening and holy Being who says, "Do not be afraid." The only time it's okay to not fear God is when He says, "Do not fear." Otherwise, ruining your underwear is the only smart thing to do.

The Jesus who speaks to the churches in Revelation sounds a lot different from most of the preaching I hear today, and this frightens me. For example, most pleas made to people today are all about receiving a free gift, which is a tenet of the gospel mentioned right there in Revelation;[7] but this plea is made without mentioning the fact that Jesus also says that the only ones who will be with Him in heaven are the ones who overcome and do His will to the end. *Talk about*

---

6. Not to be confused with some forms of loud Pentecostalism where lots of things are happening except brokenness. When God is truly present, people are broken, meaning humble. You can fall down without being humble.

7. Revelation 22:17: "Whoever wishes, let him take the free gift of the water of life."

your fine print. Jesus certainly expects more of us than our local churches do. He expects our full devotion, which in turn affects how we live. In other words, if we experience Jesus, we will do *something*.

When I attended the Vineyard Christian Fellowship of Anaheim, there was a youngish man there by the name of Monte Whitaker, who was blessed with a burden for the less privileged. Speaking with the pastor, John Wimber, one day Monte mentioned his dream of becoming a missionary in countries where the population was desperately poor. Looking over his shoulder, Wimber said to Monte, "You don't have to go overseas to become a missionary. There's a less privileged neighborhood right over there." Don't you just hate a pragmatist?

Being a doer, Monte and his wife, Brandi, gathered up some canned goods from their own cupboard and used a closet in the church to start a food pantry. Soon other members of the church started giving to the food pantry, and the janitor had to find someplace else to put his broom. Then Monte and a group of volunteers started having a traditional Communion after the regular church services where the poor showed up in droves to eat, receive bags of groceries and hear the gospel. The Communion of tradition was actually a meal, not just God's little holy snack,[8] sacramental Cheez-Its.

One of the other things that grew out of this, besides the fact that Monte created a full-time job for himself as the Pastor of Compassion Ministries, was the monthly lunch bags. The Compassion Ministry volunteers would bag up canned goods, some toiletries, anything nonperishable and sack them in a brown lunch bag along with an invitation to the Sunday Communion for the poor, which they called "Lamb's Lunch." Amazingly, we never received any complaints for not actually

---

8. My thanks to David Kirkwood for this term.

serving lamb. Then church members would grab a couple of bags each month, and when we were out and about and happened to see someone homeless, we could wave the bag at them and say, "You see what it's like to have a job? You can buy food." No, we didn't do that. That's completely the opposite of what we did. That's why it's a joke, for those of you in the remedial comedy stage of life. With the brown bag, we could at least hand them this small token of a care package.

Believe it or not, some church members were cynical about handing out lunch bags. *What good is it really doing? Does it really address the issue? How is this going to affect real-estate prices?* Everybody, Christian or not, says they care about the poor, but as soon as a church in a nice suburban neighborhood opens its doors and makes its parking lot available for the homeless to pitch their boxes, people are complaining to the city about property values, and condo developers put pressure on the city, somehow made insecure by cardboard housing. *"If I buy a refrigerator, and someone makes a home out of its box, technically, don't they owe me rent?"* Oh, they might not say property values. They might use the angle of safety, save the children, our precious little whales, and all that. But it boils down to the same thing: None of these people, Christian or not, really likes Jesus (see Matt. 25:40). And they especially hate living next to a home with Maytag printed on its side.

This very thing happened to a Lutheran church in Albuquerque, New Mexico. They were located in a residential community, and every Sunday after church they fed around 75 homeless people. The city was petitioned to get the church to stop, because the community felt that it brought in a bad element. The mentality seemed to be, "The banker who's been embezzling can live here; we just don't want any unshaven sinners."

In my own experience, I find that the times I most experience the presence of Jesus in my life is when I'm doing something that's close to His heart, such as feeding the poor, visiting orphans or visiting them when they're older and serving time in the state penitentiary.

One thing I have found, there is an art in caring for the homeless. You have to do it consistently to develop an understanding of the homeless subculture. My wife has a friend who keeps trying to care for the homeless, but they don't like her. I keep telling her, "You can't give them a shower with a spray bottle. At least, not without asking." Once, she and her husband handed a homeless man some blankets and pillows, and he threw them about in a rage, screaming about "not wanting their handouts." *Next time, charge him 20 bucks.* Another time they handed a homeless person a bag of fast food they purchased specifically for him, and he thanked them by placing the cheeseburgers under his armpits while yelling, "I smell like cheese already!"[9]

Still, my wife's friend keeps trying.

As we were walking into Starbucks today, there was a young man sitting on the curb, certainly looking analogous of a life that's been kicked there. My wife's friend bought him some food and then said to me, "You take it to him. They don't like me." Theologically, I'm not sure if you can get credit for someone else's heavenly reward, but I took the bag of food over to the young man. We asked him if he wanted some food before this, as she's learning to ask first. His name is Wayne and he's only 19.

I asked him how he ended up on the streets.

At 16, he was placed in some type of program for teenagers dealing with various behavioral issues. I think it was called a public school. Actually, the program dealt with some drug-related issues, among others, though he claims that his was anger related. He has a mild speech impediment, but you can

---

9. Actually, he just threw the food down and yelled, "I don't want your leftovers." I added the armpit thing for comedic purposes.

certainly understand him clearly and he appears to have all his mental faculties. He even ate the food by placing it in his mouth.

I talked to him about living on the streets, and it turns out that his living area basically surrounds the street our home is on. When I mentioned a Christian-based program that helps the homeless transition from the streets into general society, I could tell from the look on his face that I'd made a grievous mistake by using the word "program." Programs are what he ran away from six months ago, which is how long he's been on the streets. I spoke with him briefly about God's concern for him, and he said, "I hope He has a plan for me."

"He does," I assured him. "Bill Bright said so."

Then I prayed for him (after I asked permission). Since Wayne is a person, I assume that I'll have to build trust with him just like any other relationship. Hopefully, something good will come of this connection, as long as I can keep my wife's friend away from her spray bottle.

As we drove away, another man approached Wayne, and I'll bet this guy was a follower of Jesus too. He just had that look about him. Smiling, eager to help, holding a spray bottle. What if Wayne keeps getting bombarded with Christian love? Maybe he'll see Jesus in this experience.

The one thing we do know for certain is that however we treat Wayne is how we're treating Jesus. Most of us know this. We just forget to live it out sometimes. When we really take this idea seriously, pretty soon we're gathering up canned goods and spare clothing and starting a ministry.

Then the next thing you know, we're experiencing Jesus.

CHAPTER 14

Apocalypse Later

(The End Times Comedy Show)

*If you've lived a crappy life,
I see no reason you shouldn't die a crappy death.*

STANLEY HAUERWAS, THEOLOGIAN
WHO OFTEN SOUNDS LIKE A COMEDIAN

One of the initial inspirations for this volume of theological comedy is what has come be to known as the *Left Behind* book series. I have come to the conclusion that if evangelical book publishers can market theology via pop fiction, then why not via comedy? The theology of the *Left Behind* series is what we call eschatology (bless you), or what I like to call *The End Times Comedy Show*.

Even within the evangelical church, we stress the "now" of life so much that the idea of having an eternal perspective is looked upon skeptically. *What are you focusing on eternity for when we are still battling male-pattern baldness?* Christianity is not just for the by-and-by, but it certainly comes in handy when you die. We are told that it is for the here and now, which is very American of us. Whereas, in countries without plasma TVs, death is often the preferred state. Our churches are no longer built with steeples where bells ring hourly, letting people know the time and that yours could soon be up.

After the show one night, this comic said to me, "I'm driving down the interstate last year, right? Traffic has slowed. I look out my window and there is the most horrible accident I've seen in my life. People bloodied. They died right before my eyes. I had nightmares about it for months. Why would God allow me to see such a thing?"

"I don't know. Maybe to remind you that life is short. See you tomorrow. Drive safely."

God doesn't want us avoiding the now, thinking only of the future; but I believe He wants us to think of the now in light of eternity. But having an eternal perspective is much different than what is known today as End Times theology.

If you're not familiar with the *Left Behind* series, it's a series of novels on the End Times that never ends. Christ is actually going to return before they finish this thing. Jerry Jenkins will still be typing away at his computer. "Hold on a second. I'm almost finished. Just a few more details. What color is that robe You're wearing?"

The first three novels of the *Left Behind* series have also been adapted into three direct-to-DVD films (or in one case a direct-to-DVD-then-to-the-theaters-then-back-to-DVD film, a strategy only Christians way out of their league in film distribution would concoct). These are films about the apocalypse with *no special effects*. I think what they left behind was a budget.

Left Behind: The Movie is the story of a skeptical, hard-nosed reporter, played by Kirk Cameron. Now, Kirk Cameron is actually a great guy. I had the pleasure of doing a men's breakfast with Kirk, and he is a gifted communicator with a sincere passion for the message of Jesus. But Kirk as a hard-nosed journalist? Maybe for a high school paper, sure. (Kirk has been blessed with the Jimmy Olsen syndrome—eternal youth.)

So, Kirk's character, Buck Something . . . whoever he plays . . . Buck Naked . . . I don't remember. Anyway, Buck is on an international flight when the Rapture occurs. Now, the Rapture, according to this theology, is when Jesus returns to Earth. Well,

He doesn't return all the way. He only returns halfway. Come on, He's the Lord. He's not stupid. We weren't really nice to Him the last time He was here.

He's like, "I'm not coming all the way back because you guys are not nice. I'm only coming halfway back. Okay, I tell you what—I'll meet you in the air."

When the Rapture occurs, all the followers of Jesus dematerialize and their clothes drop right where they're standing or sitting or throwing a softball. Then Jesus meets all these naked people in the air. (I guess if you can't wear anything nice, don't wear anything at all.)

Hopefully, He'll be passing out robes. "You're in the choir. Quick, put it on, before your mom gets here."

But this is what I find most humorous about the whole story line. The Rapture occurs during this airplane flight, and no one notices. I guess they're all a little drowsy. "I thought there was someone sitting next to me. Oh, well, more peanuts!"

Or maybe they're just thinking the same thing I'd be thinking—"Hey, free clothes."

"Look! I found an iPod."

Now, sitting across the aisle from Buck is an elderly lady who says to him, "Say, young man, could you check the lavatory for my husband?" And Buck says, "I'd be happy to, ma'am." Then she grabs a pile of clothing, holds it out and says, "Could you take this with you? He seems to have wandered off without his clothing."

Now, it occurred to me, here is a lady who has been married to this man, I don't know, 40, 50, 60 years; he's a known follower of Christ; yet it doesn't seem to phase her that he's wandered off naked.

Apparently, he's pulled this stunt before. Like it's some sort of aggressive outreach tactic. "Yeah, he likes to wander off naked, draw a crowd and then preach the gospel."

"That's right, folks, let me tell you about my left behind. I'm warning you, the end is near."

Personally, I would like to be around for the Apocalypse, not that I have a doomsday wish or anything. It's just that I have a Y2K kit I'd like to get *some* use out of.

Many people are skeptical of those who claim to discern the signs of the end, and some of this has to do with their hairstyles. How can you discern the signs of the Apocalypse if you can't even discern a good hairpiece from a bad one?

This will probably come as a shock to many, but the only thing essential about End Times theology is this: You will die.

Have a nice day.

I'm not exactly sure why the return of Christ is considered by some an essential to the faith, but what I do know for certain is that Christ said He will return. We don't know when. That pretty much sums up everything we know about End Times theology. How Jerry Jenkins and Tim LaHaye got 12 novels[1] out of that, I have no idea.

The thing we do know beyond the shadow of a doubt is that you will die. (Sleep tight.) That's essential to the gospel. If you weren't going to die, there would have been no need for Christ to come into this world, let alone come back again. This makes your death an essential part of the gospel, more so than the antichrist getting elected president. For some reason, there are people who feel that the antichrist getting elected president is essential to End Times theology. I guess that's why they keep voting Republican. (Cheap joke. Too easy. Couldn't resist. My apologies.) The word "antichrist" only appears five times in the Bible, and it's not used to describe anyone in particular. It just means "against Christ" and can be used in general to describe anyone whose name is Hillary Clinton.[2]

---

1. I don't know how many novels they actually wrote. Twelve sounds like a good guess.

2. Just trying to be nonpartisan, since I did a joke about Republicans earlier.

However, the Bible does talk a lot about you dying.

I love jokes about death.

Woody Allen has a famous joke about death in which he says, "I'm not afraid of death. I just don't want to be there when it happens."

Drew Carey has a great joke about his dad dying.

Really.

He says, "My dad died when I was 11. At least, that's what he told us in the letter."

I always loved that joke because my dad did die when I was 11, which is where my preoccupation with death probably stems. When you lose a parent at a young age, I think it's only natural to ask the big questions about Death, like, "Does he exist somewhere now? Will I ever see him again? What's that sickle for?"

British evangelist Leonard Ravenhill[3] said that we are too earthbound. We think just as the world thinks. We spend our time and our money just the same as everyone else. We do not have "eternity stamped on our eyeballs." But thankfully, we do have Toppik™ hair-building fibers, which provide a full head of hair in 30 seconds. We have the important issues covered.

The only apocalypse you're likely to experience is when you meet God face to face one day, more than likely, when you're dead. Whether or not that meeting goes well depends on how you lived your life here and now. Eternity still matters. The only reason "now" even matters is *because* of eternity. Let's just hope your apocalypse comes later than sooner.

---

3. If you're not familiar with Leonard Ravenhill just imagine reading a book while a bear claws your heart out. That's kind of what it's like reading Len, but that's why I love the guy. One of his books is actually titled *Meat for Men*. Swallow. I dare ya. Another of his books is called *Sodom Had No Bible*. So what's your excuse? Another is called *America Is Too Young to Die*. I'm hoping they'll publish his complete works and call it *To Hell in a Hand Basket*. You can download his sermon "The Judgment Seat of Christ" at www.SermonIndex.com. It's a classic.

My suggestion, you should prepare for your death. Try holding your breath until you pass out. After you find that this is completely unhelpful, like I did, you should think long and hard about dying (while conscious). Contemplating death helps us in the here and now, but passing out after holding your breath only gives you a headache.

It's good to contemplate the end times, the end of your life and mine, because it often makes us more conscious of how we're living our lives in the here and now. "It is better to go to a house of mourning than to go to a house of feasting, for death is the destiny of every man; the living should take this to heart" (Eccles. 7:2). When's the last time you crashed a funeral?

Okay, let me walk you through this.

When I was a high school freshman, my mother had a friend who was a born-again Christian, the kind who kept inviting my mom to meetings called Aglow, where Christian women got together and tried to burn each other's retinas out with their smiles. Discovering that I had an interest in literature, meaning *Franny and Zoey*, *Slaughterhouse Five*, *My Name Is Asher Lev*, *Siddhartha*, and such novels, she gave me a novel called *The Rapture*,[4] meaning she didn't know literature from the Riverdale ramblings of *Archie Comics*.

The Rapture is an out-of-print, pre-*Left Behind* novel that had the misfortune of missing the Christian marketing blitzkrieg and the doomsday industry cash flow. It's about the end of the world and the final judgment and all that stuff that makes for light bedtime reading.

Now, reciting dreams is not something I usually do, unless I can share with my wife the good news that I have withstood the advances of Penelope Cruz yet again. I'm not a dream-sharer, one of these, "Hey, would you like to hear my dream? Penelope

---

4. Not to be confused with the novel *The Rapture* that Jerry Jenkins wrote with Timmy.

Cruz asked me out and then her face melted and she flew away on a piano with wings after I said, 'No, thank you, I'm married,' of course. And you were there, but you didn't look like you because you had the head of a bear. But you still wore glasses."

"Yes, certainly, I love hearing things that make absolutely no sense to me personally."

Against all odds, I still remember a dream I had because of that silly little book *The Rapture*, sans Penelope Cruz.

Before I fell asleep one night, I read about 40 pages of *The Rapture*. (Theologians generally do not recommend reading about the Apocalypse before bed.) In my dream, I wake up, which is bizarre enough because you're still asleep, but it feels like you're awake, until you wake up and then you're thankful that you were asleep. Anyway, I wake up in my dream and know instantly that something earth-shattering is happening. Throwing off my covers, I run upstairs and open the front door, realizing that underwear alone is completely inappropriate attire for a worldwide disaster.

The sky is that calm gray dusk. (For those of you who would like to reenact this for your youth group, this is where you cue the sound engineer to begin Larry Norman's *I Wish We'd All Been Ready*.)

I look up and realize that Jesus is returning to Earth. I cannot see this, but somehow when I step outside, I know. Falling to my knees in fear, I know that I'm not ready. This begs the question: If you're only in your briefs when the Rapture occurs, will people be as concerned about your disappearance? Chances are they'll just be annoyed that you didn't pick up your underwear again.

Of course, I was relieved it wasn't apocalypse now, but apocalypse later. Had it been real, the only positive thing for me at the time would have been the fact that I had a history exam the next day, which I didn't study for, and my history teacher was a

Christian. But this dream got me to thinking about my death and thinking about death got me to thinking about spiritual things and thinking about spiritual things got me to thinking about Christ who is rumored to have conquered death. You see how contemplating death can be helpful?

"If you were to die tonight . . ." is a question currently out of vogue in evangelicalism, though Jesus stated a similar premise in the parable of the rich fool when He said, "But God said to him, 'You fool! This very night your life will be demanded from you. Then who will get what you have prepared for yourself?'" (Luke 12:20). Then the rich fool went into denial, starting the five stages of coping with death beginning with denial, anger, bargaining, grief and acceptance; but since these were created by the medical community to give us a false sense of control, God took him at stage two.

In our culture, people fear death because they fear the unknown, which really shows how profoundly ignorant our views of death have become. During a lecture at the Duke Divinity School, Methodist theologian Stanley Hauerwas asked the audience how they would like to die. The responses ranged from "quickly" to "in my sleep" to "not on stage." (Okay, had I been there, that would have been my answer.) He went on to explain that medieval people feared a quick and sudden death because it would not give them time to be ministered to by the church. Armies even debated whether an ambush was immoral because it didn't give their opponents time to prepare for death. Medieval people wanted a lingering death because this would give them time to reconcile with their enemies. In other words, they wanted to attend one more family reunion.

They didn't fear death.

They feared God.

There's an episode of the old *Mary Tyler Moore Show* called "Chuckles Bites the Dust." In the episode, an employee of the station who plays Chuckles the Clown is on assignment one day at the circus. Dressed as a peanut, Chuckles the Clown is killed by an elephant.

Though everyone loved Chuckles, they can't help making jokes about his death. They all find it troubling but can't seem to stop making jokes. Lou Grant, Mary's boss, explains that it's "kind of a defense mechanism. It's like whistling in a grave-yard. You try to make light of something because it scares you. We laugh at death because we know death will have the last laugh on us."

It's this stupid idea of being afraid of death again. Death is not the thing to be feared, Lou. God is. The only thing that makes death scary, besides the black hood and sickle, is facing the Judg-ment Seat of Christ. This viewpoint makes the pastor really im-portant. Hauerwas says, "Nobody believes that an incompetent pastor can threaten their salvation, but we do believe that an incompetent doctor can threaten our lives." There are plenty of malpractice suits, but no malpreaching suits. Probably because by the time you find out how horribly wrong your pastor is, it's too late. All you can do is stand and point at him during the Last Judgment, screaming, "That's the idiot who said the Bible was changing with the times! And he's wearing a wig!"

This is why preaching is the highest calling of any vocation that exists. Preaching is the most noble of all professions, more so even than being a doctor. The only thing a doctor's misdiag-nosis can do is kill you. The preacher's misdiagnosis can send you to hell. I really don't think we enter the pulpit anymore with such a weighty attitude—my words could lead someone toward life or death. This stuff puts the fear of God in me. Thankfully, it doesn't matter how many sermons I preach, I can always claim I was just a standup comic.

The ancients feared God. Today, fearing God is rarely dis-cussed, but the sentiment you never hear expressed is fearing

Christ; but maybe this is because Jesus is always saying, "Do not fear. Do not be afraid. Have you no faith? Why are you all so stupid?" However, in the sixth chapter of the book of Revelation, the apostle John wrote, "Then the kings of the earth, the princes, the generals, the rich, the mighty, and every slave and every free man hid in caves and among the rocks of the mountains. They called to the mountains and the rocks, 'Fall on us and hide us from the face of him who sits on the throne and from the wrath of the Lamb!'" (Rev. 6:15-16).

Basically, the sentiment is, "I'd rather face an avalanche than the risen Christ." A healthy fear of Christ shows a more fully orbed picture of Jesus, because we will all stand before the Judgment Seat of Christ where we will have to explain *why* we were so stupid.

Sweet dreams.

There is quite a bit of agreement among theologians that the Last Judgment will take place in front of everyone. This means that when God judges Christian films, we're going to have to watch them all again. This is probably where the idea of purgatory, a temporary suffering before we enter heaven, comes from.

The idea behind the Judgment Seat of Christ is that our actions and our deeds will produce evidence of our relationship with Christ (or not). Everything will be exposed at the Judgment Seat of Christ. Leonard Ravenhill preaches with a passion on this subject, but not without a sense of humor. "They couldn't find the 18 minutes on the tapes of President Nixon," he says. "Well, I'll tell you who has a perfect record of them." Apparently, whatever happens in Vegas doesn't stay in Vegas. Those ads are rather misleading. It will all be revealed at the Judgment Seat of Christ where God will also hold us accountable for every word that has come out of our mouths. This is going to be a long day for comedians.

Some of the Christians will protest (surprise!) and they'll say, "But, Jesus, we cast out demons in Your name. We healed the sick. We told a bunch of clean jokes." Then Jesus will look at them and say, "And you are . . . ?"

And they'll try and slip Jesus $20, and Jesus will say, "This isn't L.A."

Our deaths should be hopeful events, not events that foster ambiguity. At a men's conference I performed at, one of the speakers was selling T-shirts that said, "Live your life so the preacher won't have to lie at your funeral." Say what you will about Christian marketing run amok—thank you, I have—but that bears repeating.

Our deaths should be hopeful events.

Unfortunately, many of us have loved ones whose deaths only breed ambiguity or worse, especially if they happened to be wearing a peanut suit when they died. It's what I feel when I think about my dad's funeral. There were rumors that my dad became a Christian soon before he died, kind of a Thief on the La-Z-Boy. Supposedly, someone walked in on him while he was kneeling in front of the television watching a Billy Graham crusade. But kneeling in front of the television wasn't unusual in our home because we worshiped the telly. Shortly thereafter, he applied to a Bible school that was located in California, and during pillow talk with my mother, spoke of moving us there. I have no documentation to prove any of this, just my mother and my half-sister Jeanie, and Bob Sailors. And the first time I saw another motorist flip the bird, my mother told me it meant, "Murder," so her testimony has always been suspect. Plus, my sister Debbie and I knelt in front of the television once during a Billy Graham crusade, but she still pulled all my hair out. So, apparently, a one-time decision is not as effective as it's cracked up to be.

I wish the evidence I had to feel hopeful at my dad's funeral was his life. If he was a Christian, it was a very recent thing, something I never got to discuss with him; but if true, it probably saved the lives of several neighborhood dogs. Truly, I hope I get to see my dad again someday (after I'm dead, I should probably add). Can you imagine seeing a long-dead loved one? I bet the first time you see them you'll scream and jump for joy, then laugh, then cry, just like girls at a cheerleading competition.

The more faithfully a person follows Christ in this life, the more hopeful we can be at his or her funeral. Actually, even weakling Christians like myself produce some hope for those we leave behind, because we serve a God whose mercy triumphs over judgment, which makes for a good funeral. Funerals shouldn't just be sad. They should be hopeful, even joyful.

Comedian Wild Bill Bauer, a road comic who was helpful to me early in my career, always said that we should put the word "fun" back in funeral. And then he said we should jumble it, because if you jumble the word funeral, it spells "real fun."

A person's death has a huge impact upon us because it is the culmination of a person's life. Death is your exclamation point. Your life can say, "She loved God!" or "She loved beer!" A six-pack is a sad thing to leave your family, and a rotten liver is a horrible way to go. As Hauerwas has said, "If you lived a crappy life, I see no reason you shouldn't die a crappy death."

You should live such a life that people don't just cry at the end. Laughter is not intrinsically sacrilegious in a church or at a funeral, but comedy and death have always seemed compatible to me.

It was the day of my dad's funeral that I listened to my first full-length comedy album. After my dad's funeral, we went to the church and had a potluck, because nothing makes you hungry like an open casket. (That would make funerals a little more festive, surround the dearly departed with choice fruit. After each person pays his respects, he takes an apple or orange, and then makes a comment like, *"Well, at least the fruit looked fresh."*)

Feeling the need to be alone, I walked the block to our house where my sister's boyfriend's car was parked, unlocked it and settled myself in to listen to George Carlin's *Class Clown*, an album I wasn't allowed to listen to under normal circumstances. But I figured that since my dad was dead, a spanking was out of the question.

Listening to a comedy album alone was somehow comforting. I could listen to people laughing without having to worry about them trying to cheer me up. I didn't want to be cheered up. I wanted to be alone. Besides, this guy was preaching. It was a sad kind of belief, really, that our lives would be better if only we could say these seven dirty words. After many years of saying them myself, I finally realized that all they really demonstrated was a lack of vocabulary.

I probably shouldn't attach any spiritual significance to this incident, but comedy and death have ever since been closely linked in my mind, especially after performing at Ralph's All-Night Bowling Center in Minot. The most obvious connection between death and comedy is that punch lines themselves can die. Some live, some die, but in a humor book you never really know which ones.

There is a punch line that I've been waiting for most of my Christian life. I keep waiting for a generation that will believe God again. And when they arrive, they will make the rest of us look like a joke. I find that people who truly believe that Christ has ripped open heaven and entered our world do more in this life because they can see into the next. They understand that even the smallest kindness conveyed with the motive of love will not be forgotten in eternity. That old phrase "They are so heavenly minded that they are no earthly good" was certainly coined by an industrialist. They have an eternal perspective, which may explain why they always strike out during the church softball game. "Stop swinging at the clouds!

Whatta ya swattin'? Demons?" Corrective lenses will not help this condition.

There are some interesting books chronicling near-death experiences with such titles as *90 Minutes in Heaven*; *23 Minutes in Hell* and *2 Minutes in Limbo*, my own story that recounts my doing a new comedy routine for an audience that just stares at me like a dog that's just been shown a card trick. And naturally, if you spend 90 minutes in heaven, you would only spend 23 minutes in hell, proving that heaven is much more pleasant. Plus, it only sounds reasonable that in hell they wouldn't choose an even number, the same way the postal service is incapable of having a stamp that's 40 cents. It's because the postal service is run by Satan.

I read the book *90 Minutes in Heaven* in 180 minutes, not that I'm counting. Looking for jokes I could use for this chapter while reading the book, that's about all I could come up with because I kept crying. Now, I don't want to give away the story, but it's about a guy who dies and spends 90 minutes in heaven. Don Piper, a Baptist preacher, was killed in a car wreck in 1989 and was pronounced dead at the scene. This preacher acquaintance, Dick, who was driving home from the same conference, pulled over and prayed for Don even though Don was dead, which is understandable because sometimes it's hard to tell the live Christians from the dead ones. Literally, Dick felt like God told him to pray for a dead guy, which is the only time you can really pray for a dead guy with faith; 90 minutes later, a reluctant paramedic checks Don again because of Dick's insistence that the dead guy is now alive.

Years later, Don is sitting at a restaurant with his friend Dick, talking about the crash, because after an acquaintance prays you back from the dead, you upgrade him to friend. Initially, coming back to life upset Don. *Thanks, Dick! I was in heaven! No more pain, no more sorrow. Hello?!* Dick maintains that he was only doing what any Christian would have done, which is stop and search his wallet, I mean, try to help. Then Dick said to him, "Yet here we are, sitting in this place, surrounded by people, many of whom are probably lost and going to hell, and we won't say a word about how they can have eternal life. Something's wrong with us."

Then Don said, "You're right. There's no Sweet'N Low at this table."

Seriously, what Don actually said was, "You're absolutely right. We're willing to save someone in a visible crisis, but a lot of folks are in spiritual crisis and we don't say a word about how they can get out of it."

Don's experience of dying and coming back to life not only affected his view of life, but it also changed Dick's view of life. Don writes, "After that he felt a boldness to talk about Jesus Christ that he hadn't had before."[5] Once they really, truly believed in heaven, they were never the same. They have what most of us don't, an eternal perspective.

In the old city in which I live, every day from 8 in the morning until 9 at night, the Congregational Church down the block rings its church bells. This is a wonderful hourly reminder of what life is really all about. Whenever these church bells clang, I can't help having a thought about the Father, Son or Holy Spirit. Sadly, most cities don't have this daily reminder any longer; new churches don't have bells that toll to remind us of eternity, chimes that gently tell of the fragility of life.

I like church bells and graveyards.

Whenever I visit the small town I grew up in, I visit the graveyard. (Hey, the town's already dead; I might as well go to the source.) Personally, I don't want to be buried in a field of flat plaques. I want jaggedly tilted stones with arches and

---

5. Don Piper with Cecil Murphy, *90 Minutes in Heaven: A True Story of Life and Death* (Grand Rapids, MI: Baker, 2004).

crosses, maybe a carved angel missing its nose with an inscription reading, "This angel kicked butt." Better yet, just a simple granite headstone that reads, "I've faced the existential anxieties of my life; I've looked into the ontological void. I've decided to take my life into my hands, so tomorrow I'm going to see my doctor about my baldness."[6] My father's headstone doesn't have an inscription, but I'm thinking of adding one: *Buy a weed whacker, so I can rest in peace.*

Standing in a cemetery that boasts such mystique, you can't help having respect for death. Much like the chime of church bells, the headstones of the graveyard whisper stories, sometimes tenderly crying out warnings about a vaporous existence and dried dandelions blowing through the air; sometimes letting on about how laughing here would echo into eternity—that you know a little secret about death: There is One who conquered it for us.

I like to stand over my dad's grave and miss him. I think about the day we buried him. I think about where he is now. I think about his life. I think about the day he stood before Congress and demanded that this damnable thing called slavery be abolished. Oops, I'm standing in front of the wrong grave.

When you die, I hope people can laugh.

I hope you live such a life that after you die people will not only cry when they think of you, but they will also laugh with the kind of laughter that often starts in the bottom of your stomach, then shoots up out of your throat. A joyful laugh, because you did something good with your life. You were a blessing. With Christ in your life, eternity intersected with the now—the Kingdom of God was at hand in your life. That's why eternity matters. It's where our country is located, O Citizens of Heaven. And when you live with the concerns of that Kingdom,

---

6. Some commercial that Stanley Hauer quoted.

you live a better life in this one. Plus, in heaven they have the only cure for male-pattern baldness.

There's this great line in the movie *Freedom Writers* where Miss G's father says to her, "You've been blessed with a burden." That's a wonderful thought, to be blessed with a burden. I'm going to start praying that for my daughter, that she would be blessed with a burden, because one day my wife and I are going to be old and we'd like to live with her. Still, I'll pray that my daughter will live for something more than the burden of a mortgage and material things. That she would be blessed with the burdens of God's heart. We seem far away from that in the Church today. We think that God's burden is for home schooling, fresh vegetables and monitoring the hours our children watch television, not that these aren't things our nannies shouldn't be concerned about. But to be burdened, to ache for someone, a country, a people—to weep God into the lives of people, that's the blessing of a burden.

So I hope you live such a life that people don't just cry at the end. If you're a blessing to others, people will cry at your funeral for the right reasons. If you're not, people will cry because they wish things could have been different.

I hope your funeral is real fun.

Goodnight, folks.

Acknowledgments

I'd like to thank my wife, Dinika, who, if not easily deceived like Eve, would have never married me. If I had the chance to live my life over again, I'd still search you out and ask you to marry me.

I'd like to thank my daughter, Eden, the princess of great joy in my life. I hope you know how much I love you, and I hope you can see, however dimly, how much I love Jesus. My prayer for you has always been that you would be given the grace to follow Him in ways that I have failed. I have always tried to convey the deepness of my love for you in hopes that your image of God as Father will always be an inviting one, someone you can run to "approaching the throne of grace with confidence," not because we are worthy but simply because He loves you so deeply. After I wrote these words to you, I wept.

A special thank-you goes to my editor, Marshall Allen, whose relentlessly annoying questions like, "What's your point here?" helped me clarify my thoughts so that they would without question insult emerging church leaders across the country. I couldn't have offended them without you. That being said, he probably saved countless Christians from being offended by persuading me to drop several jokes about a certain restaurant chain where the young ladies wear owls on their T-shirts, among other jokes that might have riled the more biblically uptight Christian. If you got through this book without being offended, you only have him to blame.

My thanks to (in no particular order) Mark Driscoll, Brian McLaren, Rob Bell, Philip Yancey, Donald Miller, Anne Lamott, Lauren Sandler, Chuck Klosterman, Sam Harris, Roger E. Olson, Douglas Groothuis, Peter Rollins, Jon M. Sweeney, Gregory Boyd, Shane Claiborne, P. J. O'Rouke, Joel Kilpatrick, Dave Barry, Richard Armour and all the other friends who line my bookshelves and influenced this book in one way or another.

My thanks to Jonathan Clements, my lit agent who said, "I think you got something here."

Also, thanks to my manager, Scott McReynolds, who said to Jonathan Clements, "I think Thor's got something here."

Heartfelt thanks to Leland Klassen, Forrest Short and Bone Hampton, because you three are the reason I'll never have to go to a men's retreat.

Finally, my thanks to Alex Field, Deena Davis, Kirsten Van Peursem and everyone at Regal Books for their willingness to embrace the controversy known as Thor Ramsey.

Un-acknowledgments

I had nothing to do with the cover. I fought them on it as much as I could, but first-time authors have absolutely no clout. I'm lucky they left this in.

About the Author

Thor Ramsey (a.k.a. Jeff Sides) is a comedian and writer who studied English Literature and Hellenistic Greek at Texas Christian University, where he nearly graduated. He is best known for the *Thou Shalt Laugh* DVDs and as host of the comedy series *Bananas*. In addition, he had his own television series, *Comedy at Large with Thor Ramsey*, which was viewed religiously by two families in Arkansas.

Thor lives in Southern California with his wife Dinika, daughter Eden and just the right distance from his mother-in-law, Maureen, to remain on speaking terms with her.

A Comedian's Guide to Theology is his first book.

Have You Had a Good Laugh Today?

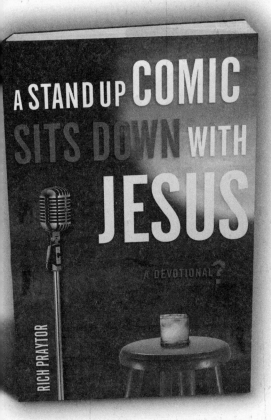

What would happen if comedy were combined with growing deeper in your faith? You would have a fun devotional for learning more about God. One of America's top comedians brings his unique style to an unlikely venue—a devotional. Laugh out loud with Rich Praytor as he looks at the humorous side of everyday aspects of life, such as marriage, money or work, while discovering something about God and His plan for us. Made up of 42 chapters, *A Stand-Up Comic Sits Down with Jesus* starts each entry with a clean, funny joke followed by a Scripture reference and some thoughts on that particular subject. Just try to keep a straight face when reading "Keeping a Journal," "Being Too Churchy", "Marriage" and "Honor Your Parents." This is a devotional like no other!

A Stand-up Comic Sits Down with Jesus
A Devotional?
Rich Praytor
ISBN 978.08307.44732

Do You Want to Believe?

I Want to Believe
Finding Your Way
in an Age of Many Faiths
Mel Lawrenz
ISBN 978.08307.44527

In *I Want to Believe*, author Mel Lawrenz ignites a latent desire that is in us already—the desire to believe in something bigger than ourselves. Wanting to provide a new language for faith, Lawrenz takes an honest dive into topics that are true areas of tension in our lives—doubt, rebirth, faith and action, and the essence of Christian beliefs. His fresh and engaging style will draw you into an unexpected conversation in which you receive concrete, concise descriptions of Christian faith in principle and real life that are shown in contrast to other faith alternatives. The chapters are skillful interweavings of narrative, illustration and biblical reflection. No matter where you are in your journey, *I Want to Believe* will fan the flame of faith and affirm your quest for believing.